# Finding Your Other Half

the ultimate game of
hide and seek

First published by O Books, 2010
O Books is an imprint of John Hunt Publishing Ltd., The Bothy, Deershot Lodge, Park Lane, Ropley, Hants, SO24 0BE, UK
office1@o-books.net
www.o-books.net

Distribution in:

UK and Europe
Orca Book Services
orders@orcabookservices.co.uk
Tel: 01202 665432 Fax: 01202 666219
Int. code (44)

USA and Canada
NBN
custserv@nbnbooks.com
Tel: 1 800 462 6420 Fax: 1 800 338 4550

Australia and New Zealand
Brumby Books
sales@brumbybooks.com.au
Tel: 61 3 9761 5535 Fax: 61 3 9761 7095

Far East (offices in Singapore, Thailand, Hong Kong, Taiwan)
Pansing Distribution Pte Ltd
kemal@pansing.com
Tel: 65 6319 9939 Fax: 65 6462 5761

South Africa
Stephan Phillips (pty) Ltd
Email: orders@stephanphillips.com
Tel: 27 21 4489839 Telefax: 27 21 4479879

Text copyright Declan Kerr 2010

Design: Stuart Davies

ISBN: 978 1 84694 370 6

All rights reserved. Except for brief quotations in critical articles or reviews, no part of this book may be reproduced in any manner without prior written permission from the publishers.

The rights of Declan Kerr as author have been asserted in accordance with the Copyright, Designs and Patents Act 1988.

A CIP catalogue record for this book is available from the British Library.

Printed by CPI Antony Rowe, Chippenham, Wiltshire

O Books operates a distinctive and ethical publishing philosophy in all areas of its business, from its global network of authors to production and worldwide distribution.

# Finding Your Other Half

## the ultimate game of hide and seek

Declan Kerr

Winchester, UK
Washington, USA

# CONTENTS

Dedication:

This book is dedicated to Fabia, Fintan, Whitby and Caedmon with love and appreciation

# 1

# Introduction

**Welcome to finding your other half.** You may wish to come out and play if you are

- Longing for something else
- Looking for more to life
- Feeling like something's missing
- Waiting for 'the one'
- Watching from the sidelines

How the game unfolds initially is by seeking yourself. This may present a challenge if you have spent time and energy identifying yourself with things that are external – things like your clothes and appearance or the roles you perform. So there is a warm-up section to see how it feels to show up in your life, and a way of checking your progress. Having found yourself there's a second game which is about finding someone else and enjoying loving relationships. Once you have found yourself then seeking and finding romance becomes easier and lots more fun because it's easier to tell what is you and what is someone else. And then there's a third half, played in extra time, which is about finding everybody else. More follows.

If you're reading this and you have limited time you may wish to try out the shorter game which is in appendix one towards the end of the book. The shorter game also provides a good introduction to the style of the game.

If you're drawn to the game the chances are that you'll have tried looking for more to life in a variety of places and you're still looking for the something, the missing piece or significant event or person that brings to you the sense of being complete.

Where and how you've been looking could be important too because it could be that in wanting to find something else you've also been looking for someone else, i.e. someone who looks 'better' than you, who dresses differently, who is interesting in ways you don't feel that you are.

So be warned, the game works when you work with what you have. You bring all of your stuff with you. The things you like, the things you judge yourself for, as well as the amazing potential that you dream about. All of this serves you.

Because finding your other half is a game it means there can be rules and directions about how to play. All play is voluntary although the game follows a sequence: to play the game of the second and third halfs it is recommended you play the first half first.

To put **a little more detail** to this: the first half to be found is the other half of yourself. This other half could be said to reside in places you do not see physically, like your sense of beauty, or peace, your soul, or perhaps your sense of purpose and the answers to questions like 'what am I doing here?'

If you want to know what this other half feels like then close your eyes and see in front of you two channels, or maybe a road or highway going in one direction with two lanes. In the left hand lane put all of your thoughts. Leave the right hand lane free. When you are ready leave the left hand lane or channel in which you are thinking and simply 'drop into' the right hand lane and experience this other half of you. In this lane you can ask to know more of yourself. Try it and see how it feels. This other half of you, the one you are experiencing in the right hand lane, this half is referred to as your spiritual self - and in finding this half of yourself you can find awareness of being complete.

The game of the second half is primarily about finding someone else, should you wish to. The focus is on loving and intimate relationships. It could be the discovery of a soul-mate or the tickle of a twin flame and finding this 'other half' does not necessarily help you to find completeness but could be described as helping you to know and experience yourself as complete. This is why the game of halfs is played by finding yourself first. To experience what the game of the second half is like try this: close your eyes and feel yourself as a ball of light. When you are ready bring in a ball of light which is compatible with your own and feel what this light is like in close proximity to you. Experiment with this light, see how it feels to merge these two balls of light into one whilst knowing that both are separate. This is something of the feel of the game of the second half.

The game of the third half is in finding everyone else. This game is optional and how you proceed in this game depends to a large part on your soul's purpose. The game of the third half also refers to the attainment of 'oneness' in the sense that you can know and experience yourself as being at one with everybody else and with everything else.

In terms of spiritual development 'oneness' can also indicate a point of development where a person might choose to ascend: i.e. having understood that life exists to bring us to the point where we have experienced ourselves the soul might ascend to continue the journey of spirit leaving the body behind. This is possible because the person has an understanding and experience of how to bring spirit into matter. However, in the game of the third half players with the understanding of how to bring spirit into matter may choose to remain in the physical world and by doing so help anchor and bring into being a new consciousness on earth. A new way of being in which we are able to be spiritually conscious within a physical body within day-to-day life. Conscious spirituality.

You can experience something of the game of the third half by closing your eyes and seeing yourself as a ball of light, and when you are ready bring in everybody and everything else as light. Keep some distance between yourself as a ball of light and this oneness of light, and, being mindful that you are a separate being, immerse or merge with everyone else and then return to yourself as a separate ball of light.

Ultimately the game of finding your other half is about being yourself, complete, and then experiencing yourself. How lovely, and why not?

The rules and directions about how to play and how to know how far you are progressing in the game in terms of seeking and finding yourself, as well as how to prepare for the game follow directly.

# 2

# The rules of the game

1. In the game you are required to be the person you really are. It will not serve you to pretend to be someone else for the object of the game is to find completeness and experience what this feels like. By definition you cannot be complete if a part of you is busy trying to be someone else
2. As you become more of yourself – and as you become more authentic – it will serve you and aid your progress in the game to allow all that you are finding into the game. This means trusting your intuition. Allowing yourself to be more playful. Laugh when you want to
3. In day-to-day life many things are determined by duality: she loves me, she loves me not; it's hot or it's cold. Duality is limited because it's either one thing or the other. In the game there is a 3D way of looking at things. You will have a pause button where you wander around inside your energies and feelings and see everything for what it is. This is called 'standstill'. You can call standstill at any time and in any place in the game
4. In standstill three questions are asked by the player of their situation. What is going on? How do I feel? and How does this serve me? Ignoring standstill can see you stuck or burnt out - unless you invoke epiphany or a source of pure light. See the rules below under 'invoking epiphany' and 'invoking a source of pure light'
5. Because experience is the key you will need to bring along your intuition to play the game. This is your 'gut feeling'. It defeats the object of the game to do something if you feel it is not right for you. (Further details about what you

bring to the game are given under the section 'How to play the game')

6 *Invoking epiphany:* 'epiphany' is a break-through in consciousness rather like a bolt of lightning. It is shocking, awesome and peaceful all at the same time. You see yourself, everyone else, and the world around you in a very different but supremely familiar way. Imagine that you've seen life in black and white all of your life and suddenly your life and vision is flooded with radiant, vibrant color of every hue. It is awareness which you have chosen to take at vastly greater speed. Few people choose this route in the game, perhaps because of the shock, or possibly because the game played at a pace where players can linger and savour the experience is more appealing

7 *Invoking a source of pure light:* Invoking a source of pure light i.e. like a guru, prophet, an angel or ascended master or light from source is allowed within the rules so long as the player is taking responsibility for their progress. This is the purpose of standstill and there is an abundance of help within standstill to help players remain true to their experience. Invoking help on the basis that the help will play your game for you is not allowed. Giving over responsibility for how and why the game is being played calls into question why the player is playing. Exceptions to this are when the player has reached rock bottom and someone else steps in to give them a helping hand, or if the player is involved in a life or death situation and it is not their time to leave the physical world.

The game is not complicated and finding the thread of simplicity in all situations will mean that you progress, even when you are standing still and it may appear to you that you are doing nothing.

# 3

# How to play the game

The object of the game is to experience completeness - first half - and being complete to enjoy the experience of being complete in relation to another - second half - and then to see if you wish to live a life of conscious spirituality, including helping to bring in and anchor a new way of being or to ascend - third half.

There is no limit to the number of players who may play this game at any one time and there is no age bar and you can play as often as you like until you achieve completeness.

To achieve completeness it's likely that you will go through a process of internal filtering, some assimilation of new insights and some releasing of ideas and perceptions which no longer serve you - all of which leads to awareness of yourself as complete. This awareness is like a gift you bought for yourself some time ago and then you hid it in the wardrobe and allowed yourself to forget it so that you could give yourself a surprise later. Dah dah!

The process of the game might look like this:

| | | |
|---|---|---|
| *Information* so we think we know | Read, experience, practice, filter, discuss, live life, sleep, *assimilate* | *Awareness* where we surprise ourselves at how much we know |

Awareness of being complete is you at peace, in balance, in joy and wonder at the world and the beauty of being alive.

Because it's a game laid out in a book and you will pick it up and put it down and life will intervene, take the game as it is laid out here as the necessity to progress things in a sequence - linear in this case - but keep in mind that the process itself will be moving simultaneously across other layers.

To put the game into sequence:

1 The game commences with each player being in possession of one half of themselves which they were dealt in advance of the game. This is your physical self. The object of the game is to find your other half. In the first part of the game this is referred to as that part of you that is spiritual, or your spiritual self. This is the half of you that you don't otherwise see but you become aware of when you recognise beauty in nature or peace in your soul. There is only one other spiritual half of any one player to be found and you will know your other half
2 Clues as to where your spiritual self resides can be found externally but essentially the game of the first half, to find your spiritual self, is played on an internal landscape
3 Directions are given to each player and there will also be guides and further help and assistance to those who ask for help. To get help you have to ask, for the game operates according to the sovereignty of your freewill. How to use guides, where to begin to look to find yourself internally, and how to release blocks and embrace change to clear a way for your spiritual self to join you consciously in your life are played in the game of the first half
4 Each player moves individually and when they are ready
5 Each player can keep a check on their progress in the game of the first half by drawing who they can see using the doodlegram
6 Upon finding their spiritual half the player may declare themselves complete at which point the game can end and the player may award themselves with their gift of awareness
7 To take the game to the next level it is strongly recom-

mended that players be complete in the first part of the game, i.e. have found their spiritual half. It is technically possible to play the second part of the game first, i.e. to seek individual completeness by seeking wholeness within a relationship with another - but in practice the game played this way round can lead to disillusion on a wide scale largely because it is more difficult to see what is you and what is the other person

8 Decisions in the game of the second half are usually taken with a full degree of consciousness and the game flows in different patterns and in a different energy from the game of the first half. In the game of the second half players are operating with a coherent sense of their life and soul purpose and are using their powers to maximise feelings of joy, beauty, love and abundance

9 Whilst all of the seeking is optional the game played in the third half is explicitly marked optional. It is played in extra time. In extra time the player finds everyone else and the importance of individuality, previously a core component of experience, becomes notional. Here the player has the choice to live life on earth or return to a life of spirit (ascend). In this game players may ascend or remain with their physical body to help serve and evolve a new consciousness on earth by living as spiritually conscious beings

To start the game: there are sequences of warm-up exercises which serve to remind you of who you are and there are directions about how to measure your progress in the first game which follow directly after this section. Like any exercise you begin to experience what the warm-up exercises are about and why they are included in the game once you do them. Practice is the key and regular practice can take you to a new level of understanding about yourself and your potential.

You may know in theory that your potential is unlimited; it is entirely different to experience this. Try out ideas, routines or exercises that are different for you and especially where you sense that they might challenge you - and then practice and play with them before you begin the games and as you progress.

# 4

# How much can you see? the doodlegram

In the game of the first half to know if you have found yourself you doodle. You sketch or doodle what you become aware of. The more of you that shows up the more of you you will doodle, and the more of you you will have found. In this way you will know when you are complete because your picture will be complete and you will feel complete. In the same way you will have a sense if something has not yet been found, and what needs looking for because your picture, or doodlegram, will reflect this for you.

It can help to use colored pencils or crayons, as color is a vibration and the colors that you select can help you to work out how to bring more of yourself into what you are seeing.

It may help to understand how the doodlegram can help you to know what progress you are making in your game by drawing yourself now, before you begin the game. In this way you will have a benchmark to remind you of the point you were at when you started to play the game so that you can measure your progress, and compare before and after doodles.

Figure one provides a structure or space to make your first doodles: you are invited to draw your physical self first, and then move on to draw what you sense or intuit may represent your other half.

You may find that as more of you shows up on the right of your doodlegram how you represent your physical self in subsequent doodles in the game can change – for as we become more aware of our other half and allow more of that into our lives so our physical body becomes more healthy and balanced and our perceptions of ourselves can change radically.

The doodlegram will reappear after the warm-up exercises, and again at intervals throughout the game of the first half.

**Doodlegram**

My physical self My other half

In this space you are invited to doodle, and make a sketch of your physical self, and a sketch of your other half, or spiritual self.

# 5

# Showing up in your life

This section is about limbering up for the game. There are a variety of exercises and stretches that you can do. Some of these are marked optional with this symbol ✡ and some are marked recommended with this symbol ∞ and the recommended sections make up the spine of the game. In deciding which exercises are right for you be mindful of your intuition and your growing sense of awareness, for the more you develop these qualities the further you will progress in the game. Your intuition is the key to your heart.

You may wish to start a notebook or journal to see you through the game. You'll find it's possible to move through the game without writing anything if you wish to move swiftly or you're reading this book in the bath, but it can help to jot down notes and insights and to review what's happening, say for when you choose to call standstill. It might also help to do the exercises where you want to be able to review different aspects of yourself later on. For instance, take the question who am I?

## ∞ Who am I?

Use your intellect and sense of yourself as a physical person, a human being, to explore who you are. Examples might be, I have these roles in life, I have these physical attributes, these are the things I like to do, these are the things I avoid. Maybe look for a short phrase that encapsulates a typical day-to-day feeling for you. I operate mostly in second gear or I wake and can't wait to get into the day. You're looking for the sense of how you typically engage with life. Let the question and answer sequence take as long as you need and get into an early habit of pacing yourself according to your needs.

**And your feelings?** Maybe extend your question of "who am I?" next using your feelings. Who do I feel I am? Examples might be, I am angry, hurt, resentful, hiding, happy, laughing, coasting, mellow, blissful, all out there, extravert - I am hiding something behind this appearance, or extravert - I feel like I want to share all the wonder of this life. Similar questions for introvert - I am hiding and waiting to be found, or I am fearful of being found or seen, or I am happy like this, knowing that I need quiet and space to nurture or knowing this is how I am.

Allow yourself space and time for these questions and honor your feelings. Read around the subject of feelings, there is a host of good literature currently available about emotional literacy and the importance of honoring our feelings i.e. accepting and experiencing what we are feeling.

Now decide you are going to go beyond what you present to the outside world. Use your intuition to answer the question in a different way. Who am I if I leave behind all of the physical senses i.e. what I and others around me can see, touch, feel, smell, taste?

**My invisible qualities:** what about the things I cannot measure? Do I appreciate beauty? How do I know if something is beautiful or if something is not?

Am I someone who receives love and gives love? What is love?

Am I a person with a soul? What is a soul and if I have one where would I find it?

Depending on how you answered the question of soul, what does it mean to be me without a soul? Or what does it mean to be me with a soul? How does this help me with my question about who I am?

You can return to the question of "who am I?" for it will change as you progress through the games.

**Anticipate changes:** it may be helpful to anticipate changes in your life as you play the game. Do you respect yourself? Do you allow time to invest in yourself and your enjoyment of life and allow time to enjoy those you love and those who love you?

This may be a good time to consider some of the books on the self-help bookshelves, see what resonates with you, what - intuitively - you know is right for you to pursue at this time.

And explore complementary means of investing in yourself: yoga, reflexology, massage, healing methods of many kinds in addition to giving yourself permission to be. Find people who you enjoy being with. Sing in the shower. Be spontaneous, be audacious. The key will be to trust your intuition and then act on it for when the time is right the support comes along.

After some practice with your questions it can help to come back to the question of *who am I?* using this question as a process. So you're not so much looking for an answer as a sense or an awareness of who you are. It can take a minute or two to drop into this way of holding your question.

*****

### ☼ Namasté

Namasté means the light in me says hello to the light in you. Think about this for a minute. Are you light? And if you are, where is it?

Keep in mind that words alone will only get us so far. I may have different concepts in mind of light to those which you are used to or have learned, so I will put the feeling into the lines as they follow directly below, with the intention that the feeling will flow from me to you.

Namasté: the light in me says hello to the light in you.

How do you experience this?

There is a glow in the words and spaces around the words so that you might experience the feeling. It would be hard to describe this feeling in a physical sense largely because the feelings you have now remembered are from somewhere else. Like a flush of love or the feeling you might have if you had switched a light on inside perhaps?

Go a little further with this for a minute. Find a quiet space and time, switch off your phone and get yourself comfortable either lying down or in a chair. Close your eyes.

**The light in you:** Imagine light, a beam of white light or the rays of the sun. Now intensify the light. Make it pure and more of itself than normally it would appear or more than you would be normally conscious of.

Bring the beam or ray of pure light into your body. Start at your feet and in your toes. Let them relax and take as much of this light as they need. Feel the warmth of the light and gently maintain the intensity and purity of the light.

The light now fills your ankles. Let it swill around your ankles and into your shins and the calfs of your lower legs. Feel it enter the marrow of your bones and from here it will make its way all the way through your skeleton via your bone marrow.

Feel the light now around your knee joints, washing them, relaxing and releasing tension, toxins, fatigue, world-weariness - we carry a lot in our legs - and now into your thighs, feeling the back of your legs relax - take the time with this process that your body needs - into your groin and around your genitals around your anus and the bottom of your spine.

From the base of your spine the light will enter your spine bringing with it oxygen and room to breathe to plump up the vertebrae. Let the light gently fan through your skeleton and nervous system, slowly suspending all tension and agitation, and bringing you into a totally relaxed state.

Bring your attention to your hips and pelvis and let the light wash around the joints. From here to your lower and upper stomach and, as the light works its way through your torso, bring it also into your internal organs, your liver, spleen, kidneys, pancreas, and further up your heart and lungs, allowing the light to relax, wash and release all tension, all toxins, and allow your internal organs to rest and relax.

Feel your chest fill with this pure, white, intensified light of love and see how every single cell in your body will be melting into this light as if sunbathing or merging with the light.

**Now bring the light to your shoulders**. In this pure intense white light let go of any responsibilities, worries, concerns which are not yours or which no longer serve you and let them wash off.

Let the light cascade down your arms, washing around your elbow joints, bringing flexibility to your wrists and tingling white light down to your finger tips.

With your arms full of light bring the light back up through the arms, through the shoulders and into your throat area. This area is where you express yourself - let the light enter and gently dissolve any blocks or fears.

From your throat bring the light into your jaw, releasing and relaxing - we hold a lot of tension in our jaws - and from there into your cheekbones and your nose, next letting the light wash your eyes like an eye-bath, and from there into your forehead where the light washes around your third eye which is located in the middle of your brow.

From your third eye and forehead the light moves to your scalp releasing tension so that you can feel every individual hair follicle, and let each follicle experience the nurture of light. Feel this sweep slowly and gently across your scalp and down the back of your head round to your ears where the light focuses to bring you into balance. You may see this as the levelling of the light to a pure intense white throughout your body. Take as long as you need.

Hold this light for one or two minutes or longer if you wish and then determine that you are coming back into your physical body.

**To come back into your physical body** make the decision that you will come back and feel the effects of gravity on your body. Bring your attention to your fingers and toes and give them a wiggle. When you are ready open your eyes and bring your attention back to your physical surroundings.

If you feel a little spacey stand up and put your feet firmly on the floor, stamping around if that feels right. Making a hot drink or going for a walk in nature all help to get grounded too.

Record your experiences and feelings and review which answers you would now give for the questions which you started the exercise with.... What is the light in you, and where would you find it?

*****

## ∞ Finding peace and stillness

This exercise is about remembering that your body is responsive to your thoughts and to what you *will* in life. With our intentions and thoughts we create our lives.

The mind is fabulous, giving us access to what it feels like to be physical, with capacities of thought and reason and how it feels to be ourselves as individual and unique human beings.

In the game your mind will be working in partnership with your other half, and just as you can bring your other half out to play so you can bring your mind out to play and you can do all of these things consciously. It helps to be able to do this when you wish to and to understand that the mind, your mind, is helping you to experience your life and not the other way around.

The mind loves playing games, and so calling the mind to play is straightforward. "Come out and play!" and it's there.

Quietening your mind, because you wish to experience something else, is either something you instinctively know how to do or you need to remember how to do it. This is an exercise to quieten and then clear your mind. It is designed to allow you to experience a pause in which your mind is switched off.

**Quieten and clear your mind:** find a quiet space and time and switch off the phone. Find somewhere comfortable, sitting or lying down, and close your eyes. In your imagination see a blue sky. Adjust the color to a summer's day – a light blue. You'll most likely find that you have a few thoughts at this time because your imagination is running the show. Relax.

Thoughts may now begin to come back in and as they do put the thoughts into the clouds in your light blue sky.

Let the clouds drift in their own time and spend a few minutes seeing how simply your thoughts can be quietened. If anything decides to leap out from this landscape always be gentle with it, let it hitch a lift on a cloud and drift on by.

Now notice that the clouds have edges to them. Between the edge of one cloud and the edge of the next there is blue sky. Focus on the gap between the clouds. Make that your focus and let everything else drift.

**Notice how the gap** between the clouds gets wider. Bring your attention to the gap between the clouds and allow it to get wider.

After a while you'll notice that there are no clouds. Notice how the blue sky is always there. The clouds are transitory, the sky is permanent and holds the clouds. This might be a good way to view your mind in relation to who you are.

Let the light blue of the sky become lighter still, and after a while of no thought let yourself drop in or settle into the whiter blue.

And stay there for as long as you wish.

You may experience a suspension of mind in your imagination and the sense that you are being held, supported by something other. Let yourself be supported. Enjoy the experience.

Once you have practiced the quietening and clearing of your mind a few times the process becomes quick and simple and consequently you can access the suspension of mind in a short space of time, within two or three breaths after practice.

This is a beneficial state of being to return to if you have too much to think about as well as a routine way of resting your mind and knowing that you are so much more than you currently think you are.

*****

## ∞ Getting into the flow

Supporting day-to-day life is a flow of life which has its own rhythms and its own vibrations.

There are many ways into this flow of life and you will have experienced the flow before, possibly when things were working out with no effort on your part and everything 'fell into place' and you felt 'in the moment', possibly you were having a good laugh with friends, or dancing and being unaware of being conscious of yourself, or making love and losing the sense of yourself as a physical being.

The flow of life for us as human beings can be defined as the giving and receiving of love. Here is a sequence in which you can get into the flow.

**The flow of life:** rub your hands together for 10 seconds. Now separate your hands so that the palms face each other and are approximately 30 cms or a foot apart.

In your left palm you **receive love** and from your right palm you **give love**. The love will flow as an energy between your palms once you give thought to the flow.

To start this flow think of an instance where you received love, maybe a hug, an embrace, a kiss with someone you love, or think of an instance when you were helped by a total stranger or were held and supported in unconditional love.

Another way to start this flow is to think of someone who you regard as a role model. This can be anyone in your life who demonstrated unconditional love. They loved you as you. You did not have to be someone else for them or seek to please them or suppress yourself in any way.

Bring this person to mind and now let the feelings of love which they inspire move between your palms. In the left palm the feeling of receiving this love, in the right the feeling of wanting to reciprocate, to give them a hug, an embrace which says I love you as you, I recognise this love for it is part of me.

Let the energy from the receiving and giving of love flow from one palm to the other.

Think and feel your way into receiving love and reflect on how you feel and let that feeling enter the flow – the gift of life – a smile from a stranger – a beautiful sunset - and let the warmth enter your flow.

You now have a flow of energy in two directions.

The third point of reference - the point which helps to provide a dimension and to anchor the experience of living within this dimension - is in honoring.

**Honoring and appreciating** is about opening yourself to light and life. You are light and others are light. Life is a gift and when we appreciate the gift we can honor ourselves and others.

Extend the act of appreciating and honoring so that you are moving the energy outwards. If your energy moved from your thought of a role model then extend the act of honoring to your role model. Feel appreciation and let it enter the flow of energy you are holding.

You have energy moving between the palms of your hands and you have now included a third point of reference, so in effect you have a triangle. Say that the third point is above your hands. Allow the energy to flow between the three points.

How does this feel?

Now allow the points to expand. The base of your triangle might leave the palms of your hand and take up positions below your physical body and the third point might move above you so that you can experience your whole physical being within this energy:

The more that you are able to focus on the three parts of the triangle - the giving of love, the receiving of love, and the honoring and appreciation of light and life in everyone and everything - the more dynamic the triangle and the flow of life becomes.

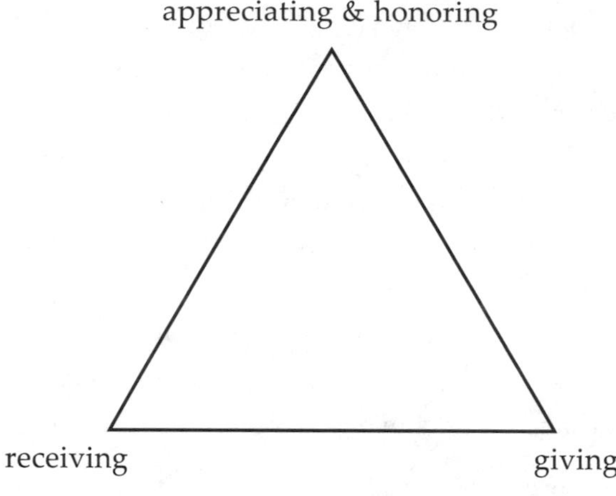


*****

## ∞ Time for change?

Are you up for change? A different way of exploring the question is to ask where your thoughts are. Would you say you are mostly in the past, the present or the future?

It may amuse you to monitor your thoughts for a day or two to see where you are because where we think we are, and where our thoughts and especially our thoughts which pre-occupy us are, can be quite different. What you find may surprise you.

**The past can be very comforting.** We can spend a lot of time there because it's a known story and we hold the keys. It's a place we can trust. We can squirrel ourselves away with all kinds of thoughts about what might have been and if onlys. We can nurse all kinds of injuries, have all manner of conversations with people and we can always be right or find ourselves continually wronged. We can turn the past into a never-ending landscape and find all kinds of scenarios in which we can live out our story and interact with others on our terms.

We can extend this life in our past to become custodians of past events in relation to others around us, of who was right and who wrong, and use what energy others around us have for past events, positive and negative, to shape our current life and effectively live a life in the present which could be described as having its core in the past.

Does any of this sound or feel familiar? In this landscape is change possible?

**The future is potentially more time-consuming** because it hasn't happened yet and therefore the tapestry can be of infinite dimension. In the future we can be who we want to be, organise life the way we would like it, and organise everyone else should we choose. We can put everything right and all can be well in our world – or we might be someone who spends all their time worrying about the future and feeling increasingly dependent upon knowing about all events, issues, characters who interact with us so that we can minimise the risk which otherwise would threaten this place where we aspire to live, but which we are also fearful of living in.

Because none of this has happened yet the future can be a place we can trust and find comfort in – it's a time zone where we can shape things according to plans, what ifs, aspirations, ideals. It never happens. Or we can find comfort in feeling fearful and then finding the reality is never as bad.

**We can extend this** too, to become custodians of future events, using whatever energy others have for the future, positive or negative, to anchor our place in a world which has yet to exist.

Does this sound or feel familiar? If so, is change possible when lived from a future time zone?

If the present is lived from a past or a future perspective how much of it can be said to be the present?

It would appear that we can shape our present by living in either the past or the future and so can live in the present with much of our energy in another time zone. Which begs the question, **what of living in the present** with most or all of our energy here at the same time? If our thoughts and our energy were all here, here and now, would this make a difference to our experience of life?

And there are follow-on questions. Are we comfortable living in the present, and in the present do we find our energy for change, and - if yes - do we want change?

Living in the present would entail bringing our energy from the past and the future into the present. Those time zones would be places from which we took learning and took our bearings but we would not populate them.

**How to bring your energy back:** if you suspect you may have some of your energy in past or future zones try this exercise.

Close your eyes – as our eyes open so our brain gears up, as we close our eyes we reduce the distractions and can direct more focus – so with eyes closed see or feel where your energy is. You can do this by following cords of thought and energy which have gone from you to things you are worrying about, thinking about, planning, reviewing and so on. Take only one thought or one cord as an example and follow it so that you can understand how this operates.

Alternatively you can ask your thoughts where are they? As you understand more about where your thoughts are and what energies they hold, keep a tally of which zones you are in -past, present or future?

If you find that some of your time is in the past or future, follow just one thought or one energy cord to find out for yourself how to disengage from the attachment that you have made and bring the thought and energy you have placed elsewhere back with you.

Does this make sense? What you are doing is bringing your energy back from where you have placed it and bringing it back from just one place. You may visualise this like peeling the fingers of the energy away from the issue or object and calling the energy form gently back home. You may find your energy has sticky fingers, like sticky buds, and you can gently peel these away from the attachment. If it doesn't feel right to do this then don't do it.

Once you have the knack of how to bring your energy back, using one or two places where you know your energy has attached, then simply direct that *all* of your energy returns to you, in exactly the same way, *for your highest good and in this moment*.

Stay with this feeling for a moment or two and assimilate the feeling. Does it feel good? Compare your consciousness in this moment to how you might usually feel, sitting with your eyes closed.

Within this space is change possible? Are you up for change?

*****

### ☼ Trust & miracles

Consider this question, if you were able to trust yourself to be and live fully in the present would miracles be possible? The question is a way of suggesting that the doorway to miracles might be the doorway we use to walk into the present moment.

If you are open to this as a possibility, if your intuition and the light of your truth suggests this is something to pursue or hold as a thought in process, then how do you develop the trust to live in the present? Does anything prevent you from moving there now?

Find a quiet space and time. Bring your energy back into the moment – how to do this is outlined in the exercise directly before this one. Now see before you a large and solid rock face to your left, and a large and solid rock face to your right. Between them is a gap or passageway about the width of a doorway. When you are ready enter through and walk into the space and light which opens before you.

You are in the present moment and in this space and light all things are possible.

Fear that I may not go to heaven – fear I will go to heaven
Fear that there is no life after death
Fear that there is life after death
Fear that I didn't go to church, read the right books
Fear I did go to church but chose the wrong one
Fear that my God is vengeful after all
Fear that my God is not vengeful but is love
Regret that I didn't do the things I wanted to

From your list what are the things that are still real for you? What of your feelings? Which of the items on your list generates real emotion, fear, dread, wistfulness, sadness, anger? Identify them.

Now take each item of consequence and highlight your top five items, one by one, and take yourself into the emotion that you feel. Drop through the emotion and where are you? Bring more light and illuminate the subject. What is it that you see?

Depending on your emotion, you could be in a number of scenes but there is likely to be a factor which is common to each, which is attachment.

**Winkling out attachments**: test this out for yourself. If you are dealing with something that does not at first feel like attachment, see if you can drop through the scene you are in to the level below. You are looking for the root cause. Look to see what this is. Draw on your knowledge of how to play the game.

It could be that your scenes are presenting to you the thing to which you are attached for safety or security. It's possible to project our need for security onto other things, like loved ones, or a cause or project we have identified with. The key is to find the bottom. You'll know when you are there.

Many attachments we can let go of. We can say simply, 'I release this attachment to chocolate and will honor my body in doing so' and it works.

Attachments which we have formed and which provide the

*****

### ☼ Rekindle your passion for life

This exercise is really about breathing... but then it's also about life, love, passion, joy... it may surprise you to find that these can all be in your breath.

Bring your awareness to your breath. **Remember how to breathe.** Take time to remember how to take a full and wide breath which fills up your lungs and practice breathing.

Then when you're feeling good about your lungs, breathe into your lungs and abdomen - put your hands on the sides of your tummy and feel your sides expand.

Once you're feeling good about breathing into your lungs and abdomen try breathing in a quality and then letting it flow into the environment around you. Breathe in love, and breathe out peace. It may help if you close your eyes and focus on the quality of the love you are bringing into your life and the peace which results. Do this three times.

How are you feeling?

To take this on further it helps if you are able to measure your breathing in some way. The simplest way is to count your breath. Experiment with this now if you wish: breathe in for a count of six in your head; hold your breath for a count of six; and let your breath out for a count of six.

Be aware of how this is affecting you - sometimes our bodies can become accustomed to shallow breathing with less oxygen. If you feel at all dizzy, because you are taking in more oxygen than you have become accustomed to living with, then come back to these exercises in your own time and limber-up for them by consciously taking a full and wide breath with every third breath that you take.

Find your rhythm. What you are looking for with this exercise is a cycle of breathing which allows you to breathe in wide and full to fill your lungs and abdomen, then to hold your breath, and then to exhale the breath and all in equal proportions of time.

**Once you have your rhythm** then open up to bringing in love and passion on the in-breath, hold your breath in harmony and balance, and breathe out peace and appreciation.

Do this three times.

This can be a fabulous sequence to do for three breaths before going to sleep at night or at any time during the day when you wish to change your mood as it can bring about an altered state within a short space of time.

Because you are bringing in and living the energies of love, passion, harmony, balance, peace and appreciation you can alter this mix by focusing on one or more of these energies in different ways. You may wish to breathe in passion for an idea, passion for life, passion for motivation and so on, bringing in different interpretations and qualities to the energies depending on your present moment.

Going for a job interview and the job is exactly right for you? Breathe in love and passion, hold harmony and balance, and breathe out peace and appreciation.

**For getting going in the morning** with passion for your life rekindled, the following sequence is a gift from spirit. On each in-breath say the following words, one line for each in-breath:

Each breath is a miracle of life
Each breath is a miracle of life
Each breath is a miracle of life
With each breath I am a miracle of life
With each breath I am a miracle of life
With each breath I am a miracle of life
Each breath is pure, unconditional love
Each breath is pure, unconditional love
Each breath is pure, unconditional love
With each breath I am pure, unconditional love
With each breath I am pure, unconditional love

With each breath I am pure, unconditional love

You can also use a line for the out-breath which matches the energy you wish to live in in that present moment, for instance, after each in-breath, as outlined above, say:

"I am at peace".

Or if you are reflecting on the discussion about where you spend your time, perhaps something like "I am in the present moment".

If you have a spare five minutes after this close your eyes and go within. A suggestion for a way to do this is on the last breath, 'with each breath I am unconditional love'; imagine you are flowing with the breath and letting the feeling of this love into your heart. Settle there and simply be. Breathe normally.

*****

### ∞ The chakras

This part of the warm-up exercises is about energy. We are all energy. We also have energy centers which can be sensed, and they are with each of us, within and outside the body. Energies can be generated and energies can pass through these centers. They are commonly referred to as chakras, meaning wheels, and when describing the flow of energies through these wheels people who are conscious of the flow of this energy sometimes refer to the chakra wheels as beginning to turn or as spinning. You may also have seen depictions of the chakras as petalled flowers, the crown chakra as a thousand petalled lotus flower being the most well-known. There are major and minor chakras.

**More chakras are becoming available:** we are making more chakras available to ourselves – some of these concern our connection to earth, some to spirit, and some are showing up with information about our life purpose.

There is an exercise for cleansing the chakras which is part of limbering up for the first game and which has been written as a meditation. It can be found in appendix two at the back of this book. The meditation has been designed to cleanse all of your chakras with some additional detail about the seven major energy centers in your body. It is recommended you do the meditation before experiencing energies that are in the game so that you get more from the game.

As with all meditations find a quiet space and time and familiarise and rehearse the meditation a few times in your mind before closing your eyes and following the flow of the energies. It is one of those exercises that you can't really get wrong because even out of sequence the energies will be cleansing you.

*****

## ∞ Showing up in your life

Before commencing the game of the first half it may serve you to bring yourself fully into the present moment in your life. You may be familiar with the thought that now is the only time there is.

Sometimes we can be 'living in the past' which feels like giving weight and focus to events which have already happened as if there is nothing we can do about this. Or sometimes we can live in the future, which is about plans, dreams, invariably where things can be different, externally or internally, and we imagine or feel ourselves happier there, or perhaps we focus on the future because the present is tough.

For now **bring yourself into this moment**. Suspend time. Bring yourself with this breath into your body. Or if you prefer a visual cue, draw a dot or spot in the center of a blank page and focus on it.

Bring all of your energy in to this breath; you are completely present, all here. If you have done the exercise earlier about change and time use the skills you have developed to bring all of your energy into this present moment. If you are visualising this exercise then bring all of your energy into focus, almost like all of you standing or tunnelled into your spot in the center of your page.

Bring to mind three questions which together help you to progress in the game of finding your other half, and which are referred to as standstill:

1 What is happening?
2 How do I feel?
3 How does this situation serve me?

Take these questions one at a time and ask yourself the questions, in sequence, in freeze-frame; i.e. you have suspended time, all of you is here, all of your focus is here, in this present point, and this too you have frozen so that you can move around inside the feelings, inside your awareness, so that you can look into every nook and cranny.

Examples:

**What is happening?** I am in the present moment and in this focus I know I can go deep, I know I can connect with all that is.

**How do I feel?** Quite different. Much more powerful, much more myself. Quite 'spacey' but also compact, focussed, it's like being in two states of being at one time.

**How does this situation serve me?** I can see that there is more to me. I can move around inside this awareness and know myself. If I stay a while I can see and feel and hear all kinds of things: I mean like situations, concepts, perceptions, and I can see with clarity what they are about. From this vantage point I can bring things in from the past. I can move them around, see all sides, I can let them go or tuck them away. I can move things from the future into this moment. I can direct my life... oh yes, and I can also do nothing at all because there's no requirement here. I am that I am.

Standstill is the key to progress in the game, a place where all judgement is suspended. Where the most simple things - stillness, focus, awareness, and connection to yourself - where all of this can come together, and a place where you can move around, or sit still, and know yourself.

*****

## Check your progress

Having done the warm-up exercises you may wish to sketch a doodlegram.

**Doodlegram**

My physical self My other half

Look to see how this doodle compares to your first, and tune in a little to your intuition to see what you feel is required to see more of yourself – and where you need to move to seek it once the game of the first half gets going.

# 6

# Standstill

Standstill is the means by which progress is made in the game. It is based on the understanding that within the game there are some things that look like reality which turn out to be illusory, and then some things which we almost discount or lose sight of because they appear to be vaguely behind the illusion – and yet when we dust them down and see them for what they are they are jewels.

**Take opposites**. They are one thing or the other, or something in-between on a scale of either this or that. When we add another point of reference, say we ask what is this about or how does this serve me or what is my experience here, we add a dimension to the polarity that changes our understanding and the depth of our understanding. In this way the either/or becomes a simple measurement or device which helps us to find the jewel that we were looking for.

For example, take the giving and receiving of love. We can receive, we can give, and sometimes we wonder if it is in one direction only, or if it flows both ways. In one of the exercises above there was a flow of energy between two points: receiving and giving. And yet in that flow there is still only a two-dimensional energy. It flows between our right and our left palm but does not fill up the space we occupy. It is not an energy we can live in.

It is when we look for a **third point of reference** that we are able to shape the energy in such a way that it can fill our space. Duality becomes trinity. In the exercise outlined above the space to move around within love was found when appreciating & honoring were added to the two-way flow of receiving and giving. As this third point of reference was added the energy within the exercise changed. This is the point of standstill: from the knowing and assimilation we can allow awareness.

We measure ourselves by duality in our human day-to-day existence whilst our true nature is duality plus a third point of reference - which here we have identified as the ability to be involved in life and to observe, and the ability to be involved in life and to experience. And to do this we are all three points which provides us with something else.

The 'something else' is an ability to take responsibility for our life. Phrased as a proposition, it goes like this: no matter what is happening in your life at some level the events, the situation, the other person is there to serve you. And you are here to serve them. This can be observation, or action or experience. This is how we learn about ourselves.

It's easier to get this as an understanding and **awareness of experience** when you try it out with something that has happened to you. So, within standstill there are three questions which players can draw on to bring a third point of reference into the game. The questions are:

1 What is happening?
2 How do I feel?
3 How does the situation serve me?

**Think of a situation**, any situation, in your life at the moment about which you are not feeling 100%. A relationship, the environment in which you live, your body shape, how you appear to others, your participation in this game, the job you do, the job you'd like, how someone else spoke to you on the bus this morning.

Bring the situation to mind and use the three questions. It may help to think of the shape of a triangle as you ask the questions because standstill places you firmly in the center of your life and your experiences and provides dimension where you can understand and grow from your experience.

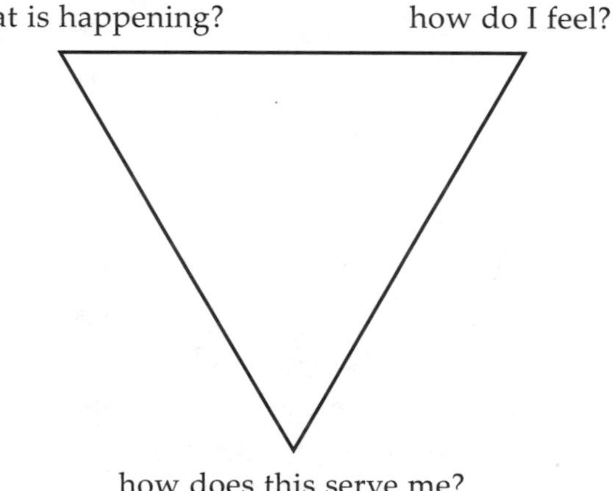


Here's an example:

1 What is happening? I'm not talking to my partner
2 How do I feel? Like I'm cutting my nose off to spite my face. I'd like her to talk first because she has withdrawn so I can see why I'm waiting for her to talk first but it also feels stupid, and I know that the atmosphere of not talking makes me feel tense inside and unloved
3 How does this serve me? It shows me I get stuck here each time because I feel unloved and something needs to change about letting some love in

Within standstill the choice to change is yours. In the example given here you are in control of how much love you wish to experience in your life.

From the discussion earlier about time and change it's clear that change can happen in the present moment. In the present moment do you wish to let love in?

# 7

# First half: finding yourself

Travelling to a wedding in Ireland, a few of us travelling together in a car, we needed directions and stopped to ask some pedestrians the way. "Oh" one of them answered, "if that's where you're going I wouldn't be starting from here"…meaning we were on the wrong road.

The good news in the game of the first half is that you are **exactly in the right place to start** the game. Nothing could serve you better. You are in the right place and on the right road. You are perfect as you are.

If this challenges you allow yourself to become open to the possibility that you are perfect as you are and see how this feels.

It may help to think of alchemy - turning a set of materials into something else. The materials you need are here. The something else is here.

To see this something else, to experience it, live it - all that needs to happen is a catalyst, a doorway, a process.

**Be the process**. Sink into a frame of mind and being where you will allow this alchemy to happen. You have everything that you need and you need for nothing.

The game of the first half is not about self-improvement; it is about being yourself. Allowing yourself to be. Everything that has happened in your life has brought you to this point.

You have the formula for alchemy to happen. You may know it as your life's purpose, the energy which informs the way in which you have lived your life, the people, situations, events and issues that you have attracted for the experiences you have sought to bring you to this point.

*****

## Getting started

You are the path to you. To find you, be you.

It can help to use devices. The thing about devices is not to confuse them with the real thing. For instance, a journey to get you from a to b is the real thing, the vehicle in which you travel is the device.

To find yourself, start with a vision of who it is you are looking for. Once you have the vision and you decide to focus on that as your goal the path is revealed. You know where you are going in the game. But the vision is only a device, the real thing is you.

Because you already have everything that you need in the game, you can be the instrument by which you find yourself. How about an image and sense of your spiritual self? The image and the sense can be found as a picture and as a presence that you can access in your subconscious. Become aware of how you are feeling and let your feelings guide you as well as your inner sight. Move either to (a) look in your heart, or (b) look with your third eye, or both.

## (a) Your spiritual self and your heart

Find a quiet space and time. Make yourself comfortable and close your eyes. Become aware and focus on your breathing.

Breathe in, hold your breath, and then breathe out in equal proportions of time. Find a rhythm that suits you.

Once you are comfortable add energy as you breathe:

1 On the in-breath breathe in unconditional love
2 Hold your breath and feel harmony permeate throughout your body
3 Release your breath and breathe out peace

When you are ready follow your in-breath and go with it to your heart. Let the sequence of your breathing follow its own natural cycle and bring your attention to your heart.

**You have followed the breath into your heart** and here look for the chamber that is filled completely with pure white light. You might see this or feel this as a mist or clouds, the white may be pearlescent or tinged with a slight blue or pink at the edge. Enter the chamber and look for a chair positioned in front of a mirror.

Go to the chair, sit down, and when you are ready look into the mirror. The person that you are seeing is your spiritual self.

You may wish to communicate with your spiritual self or sit with the experience for a while. Occasionally the image is misted or not clear. If this is the case then within your heart chamber call standstill. Ask what is going on, how am I feeling, and how does this serve me? Invariably the answers you get will also propel you a long way down your path but for the moment look to freeze-frame the moment and assimilate the learning.

After a moment look again at the mirror and open to the reflection which may now be there as a picture or as the sense of yourself spiritually. Enter in or sink into your senses some more - it's like opening up, allowing yourself to experience in this way. Go with what feels natural in this new way of understanding yourself. Be aware of what you are finding.

When you are ready to return bring your attention back to your breath. Become conscious of breathing more deeply and the feel of the air moving in through your nose. Breathe more deeply again and wiggle your fingers and toes. When you are ready open your eyes and make sure you are back fully in the room.

Record your experiences. Often, as we jot things down, things that we were not consciously aware of come back to mind.

You may have opted to make your first move a view of your spiritual self with your third eye. This journey can be more immediate, almost as if we find a travelling companion as well as the goal for the game of the first half.

### (b)Your spiritual self and your third eye

Find a quiet space and time. Switch off the phone. Make yourself comfortable either lying or sitting down. Close your eyes.

In miniature you step into the base of your head through a little doorway around the back of your head at the point where the spine comes into the skull. Look for the doorway. Open the door and step in to the base of your head, take your bearings and have a good look around.

If you look ahead you see your mouth, and then looking upwards your nose and then your eyes. Above this look for your third eye. You'll find your third eye up on a gallery above your physical eyes and in the middle of your brow. The gallery is decorated and there is color.

You have the sense of a figure and also an energy. This is your spiritual self. Bring the figure into focus and as you do this relax. Release all pre-conceptions. This is a game and you are in the mood for discovery.

If it feels right there is also a spiral stairway which you may climb to meet with your spiritual self. Honor your intuition to sense if now is the time to make a conscious introduction or if there is more you wish to know first.

**You may wish to communicate** with your spiritual self, give your other half a hug or just be. Experiment with what feels right, ask questions, ask about the wild card.

When the time is right, say goodbye, returning to the base of your skull and coming out through the little door in the back of your head.

Make the decision that you are returning to full consciousness and gently wiggle your fingers and toes. Become conscious of your breathing and breathe more deeply and in your own time open your eyes and return to your physical body.

Note your feelings and impressions in your journal.

Do you have a sense of what your game of the first half is about? It may be a feeling, it may be a picture which you could draw, or it may be a shadowy figure which is showing just enough light for you to see.

*****

## Your energy signature

Depending on how your first move went you may wish to take a journey which can help to consolidate your sense of who you are looking for. This is to experience your spiritual self as an energy and to familiarise yourself with the energy so that you will know yourself. This can entail merging your physical and spiritual selves, albeit briefly. You may have felt this already so this move is optional.

## How does it feel to be whole?

Find a quiet space and time. Minimise disruptions, switch off phones. Get comfortable and close your eyes.

With your eyes closed see a candle flame before you. See colors within the flame and allow the colors to change to silver, violet and gold. See the candle flame change in size so that it is large enough for you to step into and take away the capacity for this flame to burn you; what you are after is the energy of the light and the vibration of the colors.

In your visualisation step into the flame and let the colors wash over you. Feel the energy of gold, silver and violet, and feel the flame cleansing the spaces around you. In the still center of the flame there is pure white. As you focus on this pure white it becomes a larger area. When you are ready enter the center of the pure white of the flame.

**Inside the heart of the flame** a little way off in the very center of the flame you see a figure. This is your spiritual self in a representation which is familiar to you. Move towards your spiritual self.

It could be that you and your spiritual self wish to sit down and talk, have a hug, and other forms of 'getting to know you' including just being.

Form the intention that you will experience, for a short period at least, what it feels like to be joined together.

Allow this to be in whatever form feels right for you, i.e. it could be that you merge, or decide to hug, or hold hands. Ask that you feel for a short time how it feels to be complete. Regard this as a 'taster'. You wish to know what your energy signature feels like so that you will find your way back to this feeling whenever you wish to.

**Do you have questions?** If there are questions which arise for you at this moment ask them in this space and in this energy. Any question about the game of the first half, how to bring your spiritual self consciously into your life can be asked and will be answered. In this moment you know what serves you best.

Decide when it is time for you to make your farewells in this visualisation, knowing you can return to this energy and the feeling of completeness whenever you wish.

**Return the way you came in**. Step back from the pure white center of the flame and find yourself in the outer colors of the flame: gold, silver and violet. Feel these wash over you - possibly the energy will feel different - and from here step back outside the flame altogether.

Now reduce the flame to its original size and see how you are observing the flame from a distance. Decide that you are returning, consciously, back to your physical body. Feel the chair or seat under your bottom and your feet on the floor. Wiggle your fingers and toes and in your own time open your eyes and return to your physical space.

Record and describe what you remember or what comes to mind as you begin to write, knowing that you are sketching the route map or path back to the feeling and knowledge of having found your spiritual half.

*****

## What can you see?: a doodlegram

**Doodlegram**

My physical self My other half

Compare your doodles and sense rather than analyse where you are going and what move you need to make next in the game.

*****

## Draw a map of your game

It can help to have a visual representation of the game of the first half. Take a piece of paper and some colored pens or pencils.

**What does your goal look like as a symbol?** Consider what symbol or sketch would represent your goal. Doodle or draw whatever comes along when you think about where you are heading.

Once you have a symbol or representation of your spiritual

self, sketch or draw in the path that leads from where you are now to where you are going to finish. Let the path reflect your inner awareness. Sketch peaks and troughs if they feel right; bridges or obstacles; other figures if these feel relevant. Include animals, birds, trees, flowers if this feels right.

Is your path emerging as direct or are there other considerations which are presenting themselves? Any sense of crossroads, different paths you might take, areas in your emerging landscape that you wish to avoid and areas that you wish to see and know better because they have been hidden from you and so on.

Represent your physical self in this landscape.

When you feel you've finished the sketch, open up to interpreting what is there. The right hand side of the paper is the future, the left hand side the past, and the center is now.

Where is most of your journey to be made? Where and what are your major obstacles? What colors have you used and what do the colors represent for you? i.e. green may represent healing and growth; red passion; blue protection; purple spiritual connection; yellow confidence and courage; orange sensuality; although the key to interpretation is to trust your intuition for colors will have a specific resonance for you.

**How will you progress through your landscape?** Do you feel light and happy, or apprehensive, or heavy-hearted and tired? If you are in need of support where will it come from? How will you know what progress you are making?

It is important to play the game according to who you are and what best serves you. Does it help you to have your map out, say on a table top or pinned up on the wall, so that you can refer to it? Does it serve you to make a series of steps along the path towards your goal so that you have a sense of day-to-day progress? Keep in mind this is your game.

As outlined in the rules, guidance is available in copious amounts which can be used to enhance your developing skills and consciousness.

*****

## Guidance

The game of the first half is about developing your connection to yourself, finding your spiritual self and finding your sense of being complete.

The key to being whole, fulfilled and being passionate about life and living is the development of your inner resourcefulness and knowing. You may have a growing awareness that all of your resourcefulness is here and now. The more that you allow yourself into the present and the more that you allow the growth of your inner resourcefulness the more fantastic your game can become. The game is therefore about stepping into the game and becoming more of yourself with the ability to be the director in your life.

In consequence if someone else, either here in physical presence or someone in spirit, is claiming to know the answers for you in this game then it's likely that they are gatecrashers. There is a difference between guidance which is given for your development and empowerment and guidance given as answers or directives which seek to tie you in to someone else's view of the world.

Working out which is which is the development of discretion. Discretion grows most quickly within the game in standstill.

**Take each opportunity that presents itself** for the development of your own resourcefulness. Asking for guidance can be a tactic for delaying your game, avoiding an issue or fear, or it can be an opportunity for profound connection and empowerment depending on how you approach it.

Make an intention that you will learn from each situation or issue that has come up for you and ask for guidance to help develop clarity, self-awareness, responsibility and connection. For instance, you can ask questions like why do I feel the need for guidance? Have I dropped my question, situation, issue into standstill and had a good look at it from each angle? If I'm stuck and need guidance does this serve me in some way? Are there things I don't wish to see? This doesn't have to be laborious - more a means of knowing yourself.

There are all kinds of ways in which the guidance we need is open and accessible to us. Having a question and going for a walk in nature where you ask nature to provide you with the answer as you walk or 'be' in nature can bring insight as well as well-being. Similarly, sitting in stillness, doing a guided meditation, visualisation, 'divining' with rods or crystals, or allowing your subconscious to work out the answer whilst you sleep or take a short nap are all open to us.

And **sometimes we need a helping hand**, confirmation, someone to share the load or carry the load for a while. Family, friends, partners can be helped enormously to know what you need if you can accept that they won't know what you are thinking, feeling, experiencing unless you tell them. 'I'm tired and need a good night's sleep'; 'I'm confused about my feelings and don't have the energy to work them out at the moment'; 'I've looked at this from all angles and there's something about this situation I'm just not getting' may be examples of taking responsibility for yourself whilst not having all the answers. In other words responsibility is not about having all the answers!

## Who you gunna call?

If you wish to ask for guidance there's quite a list. You might ask for guidance of spirit, of angels, of ascended masters, of fairies and nature spirits, or of ancestors, by using energies to be found in crystals, or by going to source, universal love, beloved mother, father God.

For guidance from people on the material plane there's people like a guru, prophet, clairvoyant, medium, astrologer, visionary, healer, shaman, to name a few in addition to family and friends.

You'll be familiar by now with the way the game is going and that how and why you ask for guidance are tools to help develop your skills. However, there are some guides who are offering to come and play with you so if any of the following feel right for you they are willing to be your companion in the game. As an example, let's say that you feel good about getting some help from Ganesh, a Hindu deity. You might say 'Ganesh, I'd love some guidance and support just now, will you be my companion in the game for the next few moves?'

Here are some of the guides who wish to be listed. Others will be playing and will relate to you individually.

## Companions of the game

**Ganesh**. Usually appears as an elephant or you may have the sense of a very powerful, loving energy. He offers support to carry the load for you. This can be to carry you, as well as any or all of your cares and concerns. If it is cares and concerns you ask him to carry, he will encourage you to consider why you found them heavy. If it is yourself and a lift that you request of him, he encourages you to take the opportunity to look at your life with a fresh perspective. Life can look quite different when you ride on the back of an elephant. He will also cut a path for you or blaze a trail if things in your landscape are particularly dense and impenetrable. He is gracious and likes to be tickled behind the ears. He likes the color purple.

**Fairies**. As you might expect, fairies are an ephemeral light energy and are on the cusp or in the twilight spaces between the material world and the parallel world of spirit. This means you're more likely to see a fairy with your physical eyes than most of the guides who are companions of the game. To see a fairy go to where fairies will be and soften your eyes and take your awareness away from your intellect and let your awareness soften too. Fairies will guide you with accessing your subconscious and will encourage you to daydream and be more respectful of yourself – what you are eating and drinking and the quality of your sleep - as well as being more gentle in your attitudes to yourself. They will also bring inspiration and this is subtle, so to access their help you will need to turn down the volume of day-to-day life and material vibration. This all points to more time spent watching insects in the grass on a summer's day and looking for toadstools in the woods. In these places you are also likely to connect with nature spirits. None of these have come forward specifically as companions so these will be individual to you.

**Angels** come in all shapes and sizes. Usually we see them as light, sometimes with more form which can accord with our preconceptions, and then sometimes as color, or the feeling and awareness that angels are around. Feelings can be of warmth which fills you all the way through and of being loved unconditionally. You may also be sensitive to smell or touch. They leave calling cards if you ask them. White feathers are the most usual. They may also stroke your face or arm or simply be around you as a loving presence.

Angels have different jobs and specialities but it's not necessary to know the name of each angel or what they specialise in. The key for assistance from angels is to experience connection so that you know when you ask for help it will be there.

Angels encourage us to take ourselves and our concerns more lightly. Life is for living, for being happy, for laughing, enjoyment, living each moment; you will find angels will encourage you to experience more of these aspects of yourself.

The most immediate connection to make and one that will last you your lifetime if you choose is with your **guardian angel**: find a quiet time and space. Sit or lie comfortably. Relax your body. Direct the backs of your legs to relax, your lower back to relax, your shoulders and neck to relax, and your scalp to relax so that oxygen flows to all of the hair follicles.

Ask now that your guardian angel move closer so that you can sense his or her energy. If this feels comfortable ask that your guardian angel enfolds you, embraces you, in his or her wings.

In this space you can talk with your guardian angel if you wish as well as allowing the connection to be. Angels vibrate at a particular frequency and as you tune into the frequency and they into yours the connection can widen and gain depth.

If this feels comfortable allow your angel to pick you up and gently rock you, as a loving parent with a child. Ask to receive pure unconditional love to the little child within you so that you know how it is to be loved and to be held safely.

When you are ready be gentle but firm about returning to physical consciousness. Take a deeper breath. Become aware of the effect of gravity on your body, your bum on your seat or the pressure of your body on the bed you are lying on. Now wiggle your fingers and toes and in your own time open your eyes and come back into your physical space.

The more that you allow the **connection with angels** to be with you in your day-to-day life the more you will find that you can access, connect and communicate with angels without needing to close your eyes and without the need to enter an altered state.

**Angels are androgynous**, and can bring in a masculine or feminine energy. Because they have a vibration that is on a different frequency, to connect more securely they 'step-down' this vibration, and take on an appearance with which we will be familiar and feel safe. Your guardian angel may therefore appear as male or female, bring in colors, light or an appearance, all of which will be unique to your connection with that angel.

With angels in your life you may notice that synchronicities increase and have the feeling that you are being assisted.

Besides your guardian angel the angels who are coming forward in the game to guide you are:

**Archangel Zadkiel** is the angel of games, mischief, laughter and the art of being lighter about the business of being a spiritual being in human form. He and she bring in a light which is often violet in color, which transmutes heavy energy in or around you. Zadkiel will also help with bringing in additional energy if you are tired but need a boost to finish your day. To do this ask Zadkiel for a series of hoops, like hoola-hoops. They usually arrive as violet in color; witness or feel a number of these hoops spinning around you for 3 or 4 minutes.

**Archangel Michael** is the bringer of light. He appears invariably as male with a powerful masculine energy. He is totally fearless and unphased. Whatever your situation, if you ask Michael to shine light so that you may see clearly the landscape you are in or the nature of troubling thoughts and concerns he will do this. Similarly if you ask him for protection he will bring light and a sword of truth. He operates often with the color blue and if you sense you are in physical, mental, emotional or psychic danger, ask Michael for a blue bubble of protection and see or feel this surround you. This bubble, whilst protecting you, changes the vibration around you. It is like an activation zone and once within this zone it is easier to connect with angels.

Whilst there are many angels you are likely to connect with and have fun with during the game, the final angel who wishes to be known and to assist all players is **Archangel Chamuel**. The 'ch' is quite soft. This angel often brings in feminine energy and she works with your heart. Her energy is often pink in color and for the game she will help you to 'pimp your ride' - by which she means help you to feel more at home within yourself. She is bringing in an energy with these words, and you are invited to sink into yourself like you would a feather bed. So relax and soften for a moment, release all tension and bring in or allow to arrive thoughts, sensations and a knowing of comfort. Chamuel will also work with you to open to love and life. This you can only do when you are feeling secure and loved and she encourages you to pay attention to your comfort in all manifestations in your life i.e. when you are true to yourself your integrity is safe. She wishes to leave the six-pointed star here as a symbol for you.

**Ascended masters** are spiritual beings who have lived a human life on earth at some point and who now help others to fulfil their life's purpose. Sometimes the energy that they bring is indicative of energies which appear to be collective. For instance Jesus as Christ introduced an energy to earth, the Christ Consciousness, which is now within each of us. The ascended masters who are coming forward to assist you with your game have the quality of bringing in more energy than we would otherwise sense with 'a person'.

The first are **Lord Vyamus** and **Sanat Kumara**. These masters can sometimes appear as two aspects of one consciousness. For the purposes of the game of the first half, call upon either Vyamus or Sanat Kumara for assistance with vision and knowing what your life and soul purpose is about. The easiest way to access **Vyamus** is to write to him. Take a piece of paper and a pen or pencil and write him a short note or question, and be open to hearing or knowing, having a sense of awareness of what you can write as his reply. **Sanat Kumara** is more accessible in nature or in meditation. You might like to sit at the base of a tree that you feel attracted to, close your eyes to focus, and call upon Sanat Kumara as an energy form. Acquaint yourself with the feel of the energy and then develop your communication, either by talking or just knowing.

The other ascended master who wishes to be a companion of the game is **Lady Gaia**, also known as Mother Earth, and increasingly, she and Sanat Kumara are working together to make available and return to us a balance of masculine and feminine energies. To experience this energy send down roots into the earth with the intention that they reach the core of the earth.

There they fasten or anchor to a core crystal energy. You can ask Sanat Kumara and Lady Gaia to fasten your roots to this crystal for you. Now ask that you have the return of balanced masculine and feminine energies, back through your roots, and up into your body and energy system as far as your heart. See how this feels. When you have experienced this give thanks and ask that any surplus energy be returned for the well-being of the planet.

Lady Gaia also assists with **sustenance** and advice on how to enter the flow and rhythm of life. Connecting with Lady Gaia is via nature, exercise, breathing, meditation, dancing, to name but a few methods. Use the method with which you feel most at home and form the intention that you will connect and let it be.

**Crystals** have a wide variety of uses including healing, connection, protection, vision, raising your energy and gaining insight. They tend to make an individual connection i.e. they turn up or you find yourself in a shop that also sells crystals and sense that a particular stone is for you. Crystals which are companions of the game are two of the more common and widely available crystals. The first is **amethyst;** usually purple in color, this crystal wishes to join the game to help with the transmutation of denser energies. Dense energies are formed at times when we worry, fear, or trap hurt, anger or resentment about issues and do not resolve these feelings. An amethyst crystal will help you with these energies if you wish to see through the energy and see the issue for what it is, i.e. what lies at the root of the feeling.

The other crystal is **clear quartz**. This crystal is to help you in the game with vision and the development of your psyshic and intuitive abilities. Details about choosing the crystals that are right for you and how to cleanse and connect with your crystals are outlined below. Once you have cleansed and formed a connection with your crystal take your piece of clear quartz and rest it gently against your third eye in the middle of your forehead. Close your physical eyes and gently open your third eye to look at the future or the question for which you are asking for more insight through the clear quartz crystal.

**Amethyst and clear quartz crystals** are available from a variety of shops and outlets. In selecting the shop and the crystal, trust your intuition. Your connection and partnership will be unique and you are looking for a sympathetic energy, an energy you can trust and work with. It may help you in selecting a crystal to hold the crystal in your hand or bring it closer to your heart to sense the vibration. Alternatively you may just look at a crystal and you will know. Crystal energy is cleansed by washing the crystals under cold running water, preferably a natural stream, or leaving the crystals out under a full moon or leaving them to absorb the rays of the sun.

Connection with the crystal is by asking for a connection. Work out your intention. 'I ask for your energies to join mine for the highest good' is short and succinct. Having asked for the connection, honor the request by using your crystals in the progress of the game.

*****

## Now change your outlook

No matter what is going on in your life at the moment change your outlook to one of supreme confidence. You have the keys to a fulfilled and complete life, here and now. With the certainty that you are doing in life what you are here to do how does your life look? How does it feel?

Are there any changes you need to make? Is there anything stopping you making the changes? If yes, put the situation into standstill and ask how does this serve me? Then review your situation again.

*****

## Bring in love

There are three kinds of love to bring into your game of the first half and each is delicious. The key to understanding love is that the more love that you open to the more love there is.

**Love is infinite.** The more we ask for, the more we use, the more we create, the more there is, for you and for everyone. It's like having a ginger beer plant, the more we allow the more there is.

*****

## Receiving Love

Receiving love can be tricky or it can be a celebration depending on the experiences you've asked for. At the most basic level we could not be alive now without love.

It does appear to be part of the human condition as experienced by most of us that we withhold love, from ourselves and from each other on some level. With a rationing of love we learn to get our needs met, to favour some and not others, to erect barriers of cause or consequence so that we are defined as here and not there and can experience separation.

Perhaps in respect of receiving love we become focused on the duality aspect of love, the drama of she loves me, she loves me not, and we forget that pure unconditional love simply is. The illusion that it is absent we allow to overshadow the reality that it never went away.

It just is. It is the human drama that provides a tension that asks is it real or is it not?

In all dualities there is a third point of reference, call it the knowing of our experience, which is what we are here for. Using the third point of reference, experience, as an observation point, we can see that within duality one point can be fixed whilst the opposing point can be moveable. Love is fixed; conditional love is moveable. Peace is fixed; anxiety is moveable. Harmony is fixed; discord is moveable.

**Do you have a connection to Atlantis?** Part of our disconnection from love may be down to the individual or collective experience of 'the fall' at the end of the golden era in Atlantis. Chronologically this was approximately 10,000 years ago although time is not the issue. What is more relevant is how you may be feeling. Check your feelings on a deep level before reading on.

If there's an uneasy feeling deep at the pit of your stomach it could be you share some of the legacy from the end of Atlantis and carry remnants of guilt and doubt. This could be guilt about the misuse of the awesome powers that were then and will shortly again be available to us, and doubt that you can trust yourself to reconnect to universal consciousness and the constant presence of love in your life.

If you have these feelings it's also possible that you also have the feeling, on a deep don't-know-how-I-know level, that you feel responsible for 'the fall'?

You could get swept up into thoughts of 'well I must have done something or been an unsavoury character in a past life to have these feelings'. You don't need to go there. The feelings of responsibility for the fall appear to be widely shared; it's part of a collective human consciousness.

**Feelings, challenges and issues** which 'push our buttons' are bonus material. Using the material in the right way means we can make considerable progress. If this principle holds true then how does it help us with feelings of responsibility, doubt and guilt about 'the fall' or other issues?

Usually what is happening is that the feelings serve us as markers for the permanent qualities which attach to the other end. One point is moveable, one fixed. Using this principle it is possible to look in turn at each of our feelings and harvest the quality which we have been searching for.

For instance, if responsibility is the marker we may find freedom as the quality which is a fixed point. For guilt, we may seek an exchange of compassion. For doubt, a return of faith.

**Random accumulator!** You've stumbled across a random accumulator. Taking the next move will see you achieve considerable progress. This move will also illustrate how you can gain from bonus material at any point in the game.

The move is the development of the skill of how to examine your feelings in the light of your truth. This can be a very healing process. Find a quiet space and time - sit or lie somewhere comfortably.

Command or direct the back of your legs to relax, your lower back to relax, your shoulders and neck to relax, and your scalp to relax so that oxygen may get to each individual hair follicle on your scalp.

Take your attention to the **soles of your feet,** and from your feet send down roots to the core of the earth. Ask that the companions of the game, Lady Gaia and Sanat Kumara, anchor these roots for you. Feel a return of masculine and feminine energies back up your roots up to your heart.

Next take your attention to the crown of your head and become aware of a thread which connects you to your higher self - yourself as a spiritual being - and from there to your guardian angel, and the angels of the game, Archangels Michael, Chamuel and Zadkiel, and beyond to universal love and universal consciousness.

Feel a masculine and feminine energy travel back down your thread of connection and if this feels comfortable allow this energy to travel to your heart where it merges with the energies which support your life as human.

Ask Archangel Michael to put you in a blue bubble of protection for your highest good.

For your journey within this meditation you can go on foot or find a vehicle or other method of transport to help, maybe **a camel ride**, a motorbike, a canoe, or perhaps a fast sports car. Make this form of transport personal to you, so spray-paint your vehicle or add color or materials.

It may be you'd like **a travel companion**? You have three companions who have been jogging along with you for a while now to assist with your game, and these are Archangels Michael, Chamuel or Zadkiel. But it's your move and your choice. If there is someone else, a guide or someone in spirit that you feel brings in pure unconditional love for you ask them to join you. And ask them to bring along a torch or light to illuminate your journey.

Start your journey and take off around your body. You are looking for an entry point to your body just around your heart area, which is the heart chakra.

Once you have found this, travel inside and **look for your heart.**

Take up a position just outside your heart as an observer and switch on your light so that you can see the outside of your heart. What does the landscape look like? Do you have defence systems and barriers around your heart? Look for images or a sense of any barriers and check out whether what you are seeing or sensing is necessary and serves you.

If it feels right dismantle your defences or rearrange things so that it reflects and serves who you are at this point.

Now observe your heart for signs that it is in shape to receive love. Picture it as a flower with an infinite number of petals which open to the sun and the rain and see if it feels or looks like a flower which can open, or one that is tightly closed, or possibly otherwise defended or protected from love.

**Ask for more light** and for a conversation with your travel companions, particularly with Archangel Chamuel who helps heal the heart. Ask her to sprinkle love over your heart, a light shower of pure pink and green sparkles.

From what you can observe, see if the amount of love you can receive matches what you need in your life right now. If the receipt of love is out of balance then make the alteration. Form a thought of intention, something like 'I open to allowing more love into my life', and ask Archangel Chamuel to sprinkle your heart with more love and see how your heart reacts.

**Is there anything dragging on your heart?** Check around your heart, on the outside, for things or feelings which may be dragging on your heart. Often these can be seen literally as baggage with a cord from your heart to a bag or weight which is pulling at your heart. Ask Archangel Michael for more light. You can ask for illumination which reveals the exact nature and purpose of any baggage or issues.

Examine these weights, heaviness, things that drag, and bring them into the light. There is nothing here that will threaten you and nothing here that you cannot deal with.

If the baggage has a label which points to something which is conditional and moveable look to see what you know this baggage represents for you. What are you carrying? What is the quality which you wish to bring into your life in exchange for this baggage? Turn up the light if necessary.

Now look for cords which are attached to bags which hang down quite out of sight. Pull on the cords and retrieve the bags. Look for evidence of responsibility, guilt and fear which connects you to a human consciousness about the fall. Take your time and breathe in love and let your game companions help you if that feels right.

There are a number of ways to **release old baggage**, issues, feelings and situations which have made an impact and which no longer serve you. What you are releasing are blocks. It takes a great deal of energy to create a block and what is being blocked is also energy.

Keeping this in mind, releasing 'old stuff' is like finding hidden treasure. You are reclaiming energy and flow, reclaiming your power and your gifts. Sometimes it can feel quite exhausting to do - this is the after-effect of the release of tension. All blocks, all heaviness on your heart have been hard work and have been a burden.

**To release blocks and baggage**:

1. Trust your intuition and do what feels right for the issues you have
2. Untie cords or cut them from your own heart and attach them to balloons of love and watch them float away
3. Form the thought that it is time to release them and find the words which allow a release. Something like 'thankyou for your lessons and the return of gifts to me. I release you now, I am love'
4. In the case of baggage or issues which are conditional and indicate a permanent quality which you are ready to reconnect with in your life, ask for the energy and quality which exists as a fixed point and see the issue which was conditional simply dissolve

**To reconnect to universal consciousness:**

1. If you are dealing with a heaviness which feels like responsibility for the fall, bring the heaviness into the light. Let it take the form which it symbolises or in which it appears to you. Say within your meditation 'I dissolve all responsibility for the fall and direct that the quality of freedom be returned to me for I am love'
2. For heaviness which you have seen or felt as guilt, bring the weight and baggage up into the light of your truth and say 'I dissolve all guilt and direct that the quality of compassion be returned to me for I am love'
3. For heaviness and the baggage of doubt, bring this into the light and say 'I dissolve all doubt and direct that the quality of faith be returned to me for I am love'

If cords are proving hard to untie or dissolve, ask for more light, and in this light ask to know why they are sticking or what it is you wish to learn from the situation. These are your gifts! It is possible to ask Archangel Michael to cut cords from you to other people, places, situations and issues etc, but within the game you will want to take maximum advantage of the learning which associates with any releasing that you do, so understand how the issue has served you before you release.

You may wish to end the meditation at this point and if you do then resolve to find time to repeat the meditation so that at this point you can continue.

Within your meditation you are outside your heart. You have cleared away defence and protection systems from around your heart which no longer serve you and you have released and had the return of power and gifts from issues, beliefs, situations, other people which previously had weighed on your heart.

Now look **for the entrance to your heart**. Be mindful of your landscape - with the release of baggage it may look different already. Enter into your heart and be observant about your environment. Journey further into your heart until you reach a point which you will know as your still center. Here there is only pure white light and love.

In this space make your intention to open to love and to open to your connection with the divine. Bring forward a form of words which is simple and reflects who you are: something like 'I open to allowing love in my life'.

Stay with the feeling of this for as long as you wish and then proceed to return from the meditation back to your physical form by tracking back along the route you have taken.

**At this point** come out of your heart and find yourself as the observer outside your heart. Find the vehicle or method of transport you used and with your travel companion return to the point from where you started. Here give your companion a hug and thank them for their help. And now determine to return back to your physical environment. Take your time with this. Feel your feet on the floor and your bum on the seat of your chair or the bed or floor underneath you if you are lying down. Wiggle your toes and fingers. Cup your eyes with your hands and gently open your eyes and, using your hands as a shield, adjust your eyes.

Take a drink of water, go for a walk, record your meditation and experiences. Avoid rushing into your material life again and be mindful of the return of energy and gifts which you are assimilating.

*****

## Love for-giving

The absence of forgiveness is the absence of love. We are withholding love, finding ourselves hurt, or stuck, or somehow blocked.

Giving love is about forgiving. It is love for giving, i.e. we stop being conditional. We give love and do not withhold, either for ourselves or for others. It can often be the case that the person we find it hardest to allow love to flow to for giving is ourself.

In any act of forgiving forgive yourself as well. If you think about giving love as forgiving it means somewhere there was a block that we put in place to stop the flow in the first place. This block also needs to be healed and when we forgive ourselves this block can be dissolved - and will not go back up thereafter.

You can experience this for yourself. Pick an easy target first of all - someone who has annoyed you but not too much, who maybe bumped into you on the street without looking or was pre-occupied and didn't pay you any attention – we like to know we exist!

Bring the situation to mind. Go back into a sample of the feeling of it and get a quick reminder of how you felt. Now drop through the feeling i.e. allow yourself to sink through the feeling down to the level which lies below. What is this feeling? When is the last time you had this feeling? What does it bring to mind? Is this the level at which love for giving needs to happen or do you need to drop down another level? – trust yourself, you will know.

**Who needs love?** If it's necessary to drop another level then drop through. If you are here where the hurt is, who is in need of love? Give it to them. Now how do you feel? If the person who needed love was not you, what about your feelings on this level below the level of the most recent hurt? Do you need love? If yes, give yourself the love that you did not receive previously. Allow it to flow and let go of tears, anger, frustration, relief, laughter. Let it go and let love flow to you and anyone else in your scene who needs love.

Now come back to the level above, the incident with which you started. How does it look and feel now? Does anyone here need love? Let them have it!

Check how you are feeling. Now think of someone who is really quite a challenge for you, a parent perhaps, a sibling or intimate partner at a time when things didn't work out in the ways you'd hoped for at the outset. And apply the process of love for giving.

*****

## Love to appreciate

Think of a role model - anyone from your childhood, youth or adult years - who represents qualities and a way of life, attitude or just being that you aspire to or admire.

Having thought about them, bring them more clearly into your consciousness. Feel as if you can almost reach out and touch the essence of what it is that they brought into your life.

Now appreciate and honor them. Honor the love in them that resonates with the love in you. And feel a flow between you.

In this frame of mind think about the blessings in your life, the kindness of strangers, the beauty in nature, a glass of water, the smile from a loved one, a meal cooked with loving kindness, a song on the radio where the words are reaching out to you, describing your feelings, your experience.

Experiment with these feelings when you move about your life. Look at a total stranger and say to yourself 'the light in me says hello to the light in you' and observe what happens and what you feel. Now widen your experimentation and do this in a variety of situations, somewhere possibly where you might otherwise feel disempowered or where it pays to be on your guard.

Once you have the feeling of appreciating and honoring, the phrase 'the light in me says hello to the light in you' can be shortened to 'namasté'. If you send this thought out to each and every person you meet, what happens in your world? You might like to experience this.

**And what of yourself?** You have asked your heart to open to love for forgiving yourself; are you ready to honor the light and life within you? How do you want to do this?

Be conscious of how you are feeling and if there are issues which the thought of honoring yourself is raising then go back into receiving love and love for forgiving before making your next moves.

The quickest way to check out honoring yourself is to find a mirror and say, looking steadily into your eyes and holding your gaze, 'I honor the light and life within you'.

See how you are feeling and what this statement brings up for you. If there is a heaviness around your heart return to the section on receiving love and check out this issue so that you can have the return of your sense of yourself.

If there are things you wish to talk about **with a guide** then sense who you wish to speak to. This can be anyone you choose. Find a quiet time and place, sit or lie comfortably, switch off phones and close your eyes.

Take you roots down to Lady Gaia and Sanat Kumara and ask them to anchor you at the core of the earth. From the crown of your head renew your connection with all the great beings of love and light and beyond to source and universal consciousness. Ask Archangel Michael to put you in a blue bubble of protection through which only energies for your highest good may pass.

In your meditation take a stroll through a meadow. See a bridge over a stream and when you are ready cross the bridge. On the other side you see a building, simple and elegant. Within the building is your guide.

When you are ready enter the building and **approach your guide**. Sit and talk, or simply allow yourself to be. When you are ready return the way you came, leaving the building, crossing the bridge and coming back through the meadow to the place where you started.

Make the intention that you will return to your physical body and become aware of the seat under your bum or your body outstretched and wiggle your fingers and toes, opening your eyes gently and come back into your physical space.

Record the conversation or awareness you had in the meditation. As you write so things which you had forgotten or which were impressions can come more readily to mind. Know that you can return to this meditation for guidance at any point you choose.

*****

## Play your wildcard

Your wildcard can be played at any point where you would like a breakthrough or insight into a situation in which otherwise you feel stuck. Your wildcard summons up the powers of your guides and the answer to your question will be provided for you either there and then, or if not immediately then in the next conversation you have, or the next headline in a newspaper you see, or voice on the radio or t.v.

*****

## Love in trinity

When all three aspects of love - love to receive, love for giving and love to appreciate and honor - are brought together profound shifts take place alongside wonderful healing.

Receiving and giving love provide a flow in life. When the flow is happening you feel in the present moment – and similarly when we block the receipt or giving of love we knock ourselves out of the moment and out of the flow.

The importance of love to honor when combined with receiving and giving love is to provide dimension:

Imagine a room where the doors and windows haven't been opened for days and the temperature is hot and the sun is shining on the room and then you suddenly open a window in the room into a fresh cool breeze.

Or imagine music playing and you turn up the volume and dance with the rhythm and move with your intuition and feel profoundly free and also present at the same moment.

Or imagine a **full blue moon**, the night full of promise which is also with you here, now, all in this moment.

And this being the game of halfs you can bring love in trinity here into your game to experience as often as you want. Indeed, if it's that good why not live in it?

**Form a triangle.** Start with the palms of your hand left and right to form the base of the triangle. In your left you receive love, in your right you have love for giving. It may help to turn the palms towards each other and keep them your body width apart.

Focus on the feeling of receiving love in your left palm and send the love for giving to your right, and the love for giving from your right back to the love to receive in your left. Feel a flow of love build up between the two palms.

**To add dimension** bring your focus to just in front of your third eye. Use the words or feelings which bring honoring to life for you. This could be how you see your role model, it could be the words 'the light in me says hello to the light in you', it could be namasté or the feeling of honoring that you have built up.

Make the intention that the flow of energy will now flow from the base of your triangle to the top or apex of the triangle and back round again in an equal flow. Once you have experienced this energy and have an equal flow make the intention that you will step into it, so widen and deepen the base of your triangle and raise the top and bring this energy all around you.

Experiment with this energy in other ways. Create the focus for the energy with candles or other markers which can give you a clear physical space and place a chair inside the space and sit on it. Perhaps you'd like to get some like-minded friends together and form a group space?

To live in this energy bring the energy into your heart. You may want to allow time for a little ceremony and use a short statement of intent.

**You can intensify this feeling** - build up the triangle of energy in front of you using your palms and a point in front of your third eye. Once you have the flow say 'I open my heart to love to receive, I open my heart to love for giving, I open my heart to love to honor'. Intensify the feeling within your triangle and reduce the size of your triangle so that you can move it smoothly into your heart with the intention 'I now direct that I live my life in the fullness of love'.

Record how you are feeling and take time within this energy to form other intentions about your life.

As with any energy system, check the love you are experiencing from time to time or incorporate thinking about it once a week into a routine that gives you a treat, makes you smile, and reminds you that you are in the fullness of love.

If the energy drops it's most likely that other issues are being flagged up for clearing. Look to see where this is and use the exercises to clear and return your gifts.

*****

## Releasing in freefall

This page has been channelled by guides of the game.

"Where it all began is moot. It can help to have the sense of a spiral. All things start and end here. Time is formless, it is a helpful tool for living in a physical plane but will take you no further.

It is possible for you to look over the edge into this spiral. You will see energies that remind you of images where babies plunge into the water and start to swim. It is natural. Drop a thought into the energies of this spiral and see what happens to your thought.

Now allow yourself to slip over the edge and join your thought.

The spiral evolves slower than a merry-go-round and you can come back from these spiral energies any time you choose. Umm, maybe it's more like floating without gravity?

Within the spiral the colors you need at this time are entering your aura, the energy field around you. Close your eyes and feel the colors, a little like a harlequin's costume. Chequered, patchwork, smocked. Yellow, blue, green and red. Now russet shades of orange, earth-red, brown and gold. Now shades of violet-blue and purple, and purple-white.

It is like being dipped into a swirling wheel that makes candyfloss, your aura is collecting colors and making patterns. Close your eyes and sense what is happening if you wish.

In this freefall you are experiencing faith, in yourself and your own innate abilities and in the free flow of the universal consciousness from whence all things came.

Do you have a fear you wish to dissolve in this spiral? That there will not be enough? That you will be left behind? That the veils you have taken will not shift and you will be stuck as a human?

Whatever your fear you have no need to voice it, simply bring the thought as a thought or as an image with density to the place in front of your third eye and let the energy of the freefall spiral wash through and dissolve it.

In the space where your thought or image was inspect the space now to see it is clear.

Now accept if you will a star of luminous quality and place this where previously the thought or image resided.

Make use of this spiral as often as you wish, it is here for you.

We wish you smiles in your games and a fair wind behind you."

*****

## Eternal truths

Duality is a world of illusion, things are one thing or another, life is conditional, there is plenty or there is scarcity, there is love or fear and so on.

Trinity is bringing ourselves into the illusion and seeing it for what it is, what the game is. We are the observer. Being inside the drama as participant and observer does not make it less enjoyable but more so. We appreciate the illusion and the drama but our life no longer depends upon it. We are not attached to any particular outcome.

We know ourselves to be love on earth, capable of observing and directing amazing energies. There is no need to be coy about this.

There are also eternal truths about our nature and purpose here on earth. Some of this has been hinted at. There is pure unconditional love. There is pure peace. There is pure harmony. These things are made conditional only by our interest in the drama. Behind the scenes – or more accurately  creating the structure so that the illusion may be played out - they are permanent.

**Love, peace and harmony** make up a triangle which matches the energy of the love triangle you have experienced. It is a gift from universal consciousness, a basic building block for the universe and for our experience of how it is to be a spiritual and human being.

You can assemble the triangle of love, peace and harmony and experience this for yourself. Start with peace and harmony at the base of the triangle, and unconditional love at the top or apex.

Because the triangle is a gift from universal love or universal consciousness it may make sense to view the triangle as upside down, i.e. the top or apex of the triangle, unconditional love, is pointing downwards.

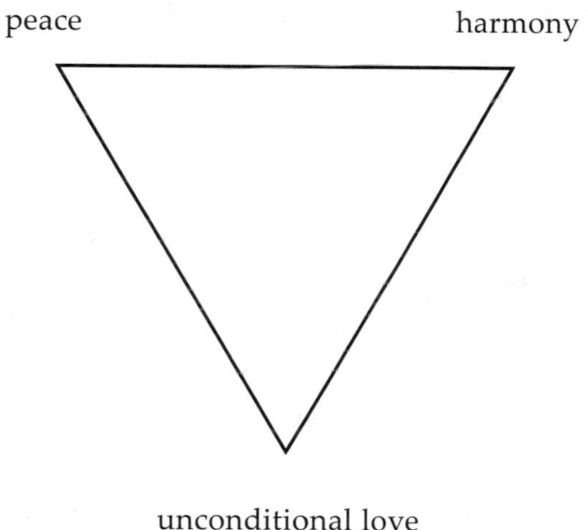


The triangle which exists as a mirror to love, peace and harmony is the triangle of love to receive, love for giving and love to honor.

*****

## The Seal of Solomon

When we bring together the triangles of peace, harmony, and

unconditional love from spirit, and the triangle of love which holds the qualities and energies of love to receive, love for giving and love to honor and appreciate then it is possible to create a six-pointed star shape, which is the form of the Star of David or the Seal of Solomon.

To construct this shape begin with the earth triangle and create the energy of love to receive, love for giving and love to appreciate and honor between your palms and the point in front of your third eye.

When you have this triangle and the love is flowing, direct that the triangle of divine universal consciousness descend.

Take your time with this experience. You may find as the triangles move into proximity with each other that there is a **bridge of energy** which builds between them. This is the merging of spirit and matter, the bringing together of heaven and earth.

When you are ready allow the triangles to merge, a little in front of you, and then direct that these energies embrace you and experience how this feels.

It may interest you to construct these triangles physically, using candles or physical markers and experience how it is to sit within these energies. The seal can be used for the most remarkable healing including release of old issues and emotions, patterns, beliefs and fears. The seal is great fun to do with a group of people and can be used to bring inspiration and healing to individuals, can be set around a house or space, and can be used for whole communities.

*****

## Merging your physical and spiritual self

The time to merge your physical and spiritual self, to reclaim your power and find your other half is fast approaching. Take a moment first to review where you are on your map.

Within the game you have been experiencing a **different level**

**of consciousness** and so your map is likely to look quite different to you now. Assess how far along you have come and determine how far you'd like to go with your next move.

It may help you to redraw a section of your map, i.e. work out where you are from your original map and then, using your new powers, draw what the rest of your route looks like.

Use the help that is available to you to assess any remaining barriers or obstacles. These include standstill, guides and companions of the game, as well as your knowledge of what works for you when releasing old issues and energies around you, blocked or otherwise, which no longer serve you.

Keep in mind that in reality there is no map to you; **you are the path**. Everything is here. It is all a question of waking up to who you are and deciding to switch that on.

Be mindful too of how you are feeling. You are in the drama and you are the observer, and the level of immersion in the wonder of life is your choice. How cool is that. Directing the film of your own life.

So how far do you want to go?

*****

## Who you are

Keep the shape of triangles in your mind.

You are the physical product of male and female energies here on earth. One and two make a third who is one and also separate. This is the basic building block of creation: at one with all that is and separate so that we can experience how it is to be.

As above, so below, you are also a product of **masculine and feminine** energies in spirit. This is mother and father in spirit, you may know them as beloved mother, father God. One and two makes a third, and this third is one but also separate.

You are an amazing spiritual being in human form. Welcome.

In your own time experience how it is to be you.

Start by constructing your earth triangle. This is you in physical being. In your left palm feel the feminine energy which brought you into being, and in your right palm the masculine energy which brought you into being. Let the energy between your palms develop and flow.

At the point in front of your third eye see yourself forming as a human energy form. Go back and locate the point at which you came into being as a human. Locate the essence of that energy and the intention which you brought with you into this life and bring it into your triangle at the apex, or point of the triangle, which is pointing upwards. Sense how this energy is as one with the feminine and masculine energies and also new. **Creation.**

Stay with this feeling of being yourself in a moment of creation for a while. Allow in the sense of wonder, beauty, joy, truth and love.

When you are ready direct that the triangle in spirit which represents your **spiritual creation** descend. This triangle is inverted so the base is held by divine feminine and divine masculine energies, and the peak of the triangle which is pointing downwards is you as a spiritual being.

Sense the flow of feminine and masculine spiritual energies and the creation of you as a new spiritual being, separate and one. Go back in your awareness to the time and the energy in which you were created in spirit and bring that energy into the apex, the point of the triangle which is now pointing down towards you.

When you are ready direct that the triangles move into closer proximity and sense the energy that builds between them whilst they are moving closer but not yet touching.

The energy which is building as a **bridge** between the two triangles is important for this is a large part of who you are. You are physical and spiritual, a bridge between spirit and matter. Allow this bridge to build.

If you are experiencing any resistance to these energies one of two things may be happening. First it may be that you wish to surrender to this process – which is allowing yourself to be yourself – or it may be that you wish to resolve other questions and issues before proceeding, in which case drop gently out of the energy and into standstill.

If there is a process of **surrender** you wish to undertake then consider first what this entails. Surrender is a letting go of something that you have, up until this point, resisted with all your will, and then embracing the very thing you have resisted.

It could be that you are resisting how powerful or how wonderful you are? It could be you are resisting the whole concept of spirit, universal consciousness, divine mother and father, that you too are divine?

Within the energies of yourself as physical and spiritual in creation, you will know all of this and more. Look to see how you are reacting to the proximity of the triangles and let your intuition guide your next moves, either to direct that the triangles merge, or that within these energies you identify resistance which you are clear you wish to surrender, or you wish to gently drop out of these energies and in your own time into standstill. Standstill asks the three questions, what is going on, how am I feeling, and how does this situation serve me?

If this is the time for you to merge then allow the triangles to meet a little above and in front of you in the same way as you experienced the triangles which comprise the Seal of Solomon.

Let these energies be for a moment. **There is no rush.** You are assimilating or re-assimilating how it feels to be complete within your conscious awareness. Unless you have given yourself the gift of ascending in a previous lifetime this is brand new and is available to you at this time because you have asked for this experience.

## Now make yourself at home!

Following your intuition, which has changed but which you can locate in the same place on a slightly altered vibration, bring the energy of you as a physical being and you as spiritual being who have now merged, this new, six-pointed star into your heart.

Form a sense of words for the occasion, something like 'I open my heart and my soul to a new awareness of myself as a complete and amazing being. I live my life in conscious fulfilment of my deepest dreams. I am that I am, I am love, I am light, I am at one with all that is.'

You will find that the right words for you pour from your heart. You may also wish to bring in your guides, companions and other great beings of light who have helped you to this wonderful experience of you, for love loves to love, and love loves to celebrate, and thank them.

This is the end of the first half of the game. You may wish to check your doodlegram or simply take time to enjoy this new sense of being at one with yourself.

**Doodlegram**

My physical self                    My other half

Namasté

8

# Second half: finding someone else

If you are entering the game at this point without first finding yourself be warned, it may be hard going because it is difficult to see what is you and what is another when you are without a sense of being complete. This is not to say it can't be done.

**Taking responsibility for your life,** for all actions, all situations, all issues, your environment and particularly who else is around in your world, this is the key to fulfilment when finding someone else.

When you have done this you know you don't need someone else in your life. That your life will be fulfilled without a 'significant other' or, in other scenarios, if you were counting on someone to be around and they walk out of your life, that you will not fall apart. The game of the second half is not a rescue drama, but about informed and conscious living.

More directly you will find if you have not played the game of the first half that the game in here does not make a great deal of sense. Your vibration will be different.

As for the game of the second half and partners, it is fine for your partner to look at these games and to decide it is not for them. It means it is not for them, not that you are not for each other. The game of the second half is about you finding someone else so that you can appreciate all that you are.

So reading this book and finding completion in the first game does not mean you have to convert your partner to play the game, nor give up on them because they won't, or give up on them because they are getting different results.

## What is a successful loving and intimate relationship?

This is a good time to find your journal again. Just when you were celebrating finding yourself, bang, here's the homework.

But isn't it just the greatest feeling, this being complete?

And it is fabulous to find someone who you wish to share that sense of being alive with.

Is there such a thing as a successful relationship, and, if there is, what is a successful relationship? Take stock of how you respond and what you feel about these questions.

Successful and unsuccessful as categories are of limited use if we take a broader view that everything that has happened in our lives has got us to this point and we are responsible for all of the key decisions and consequences. In this sense every relationship is successful, it brings to us what we have asked for.

It may be useful to see how this has worked for you in your life so far.

Jot down the things that you have done or have experienced that you **do not want** in a relationship again. Base this on your own experience, either where you were within a relationship or where you have observed a relationship, say your parents, and the elements that you do not want will stand out quite starkly. Trust your intuition.

Below are some examples; you'll benefit from this exercise when you use things that are true to you. It doesn't matter if these are things that you brought to the relationship, or that your partner brought to the relationship, or things that were created because you were together, or things you have observed about other relationships. Write down the things you do not want.

***Don't want***

Not being honest

Pretending to be someone I'm not

Thinking s/he will fix the gaps

Thinking that if I love her/him enough things will come right

Disrespect of any kind
Disinterest
Lack of loving communication
Sulks and other forms of manipulation
Not being able to stand up for myself – and/or having to stand up for myself on a constant basis
Not being loved
Feeling I have to make the other person happy
A partner who doesn't know what they want

The more authentic and true to your experience you can make it the better it gets. As you can see from the list above it doesn't matter who contributed what, simply write it down.

Next, take the notes you made to the first question and turn them around as if you were talking about yourself:

| ***Don't want*** | ***I do want*** |
|---|---|
| Not being honest | To be honest |
| Pretending to be someone I'm not | To be authentic |
| Thinking s/he will fix the gaps | To be complete |
| Thinking that if I love her/him enough things will come right | To love myself |
| Disrespect of any kind | To respect myself |
| Disinterest | To be interested |
| Lack of loving communication Sulks/manipulation | To communicate with love, not hurt |
| Not being able to stand up for myself – and/or having to stand up for myself on a constant basis | To have no barriers/conditions |
| Not being loved | To be confident and lovingly assertive |

| | |
|---|---|
| Feeling I have to make the other person happy | To love myself<br>To be happy and self-contained |
| A partner who doesn't know what they want | To know what I want |

The list now is about you. These are qualities that you wish for for yourself. Check your list to see if it is authentic for you.

As you can see, relationships hold up to us a mirror in which we see the qualities we wish to bring into our lives and those aspects of ourselves which we wish to experience. All relationships, those you have actively sought and those where you might describe yourself as observing more than actively choosing, have brought to you the gifts that you have sought in life.

The key is to **be the change you wish to see** and then your partner has space to change and to be more of themself. That's simply how the energy works. If they are not ready to be more of themselves you will part, unless you are choosing to stay together because this is 'right' for you. 'Right' and 'wrong' do not carry judgement – they simply match what you now choose to experience and what you do not. It may be more accurate to say this serves me, this does not. And it can serve us to remain in what might appear to be a dysfunctional relationship just as it can serve us to leave one. You will know.

**If you are not in a relationship,** by making the changes you will attract a partner who can help you with your list or will match your list with amazing accuracy. But also be clear that your list is changing and allow space for the change, in other words allow space for you.

For now review your list of what you do want and check out how much of this is still relevant. It may help to rank your points in some kind of order, say your top five, and make a shorter list of these.

If you find your energy is flagging or you are not clear how you are feeling about some of the items on your list, don't worry. We spend a lot of time finding fault with each other and with ourselves and the energy that surrounds the finding of fault is particularly dense. It holds us and gets us stuck.

The best antidote to this is to drop into standstill and work out what the benefits are to you of holding yourself back in this way. How does the situation serve you? It could be you are here to experience a profound shift in personal responsibility and it's only by building up sufficient energy behind the issue – picture a temporary block in a river - that you will generate the will to do something about it and move forward.

After standstill bring yourself back within your own knowing and your own power. Get back to your whole self through the breath.

**To bring in your completeness**: breathe in 'I am love', hold your breath and experience 'I am harmony' and release your breath with 'I am peace'. Do this sequence for three breaths and on your fourth breath, 'I am love', slip gently into your heart and into the star that represents you as created on earth and created in spirit. Here you are yourself as human and yourself as divine spirit. You have merged these in your heart and you now direct that the energy of your completeness infuse and inform the whole of yourself. This takes a minute or two.

Now return to your conscious self and experience how you are feeling.

Any time that you find yourself wanting to become more of yourself, come back to the exercise of bringing in your completeness and make the conscious decision to raise your vibration. To raise your vibration allow more love in. Be light.

**After a while the new you will be you** and you'll find there isn't a great change, more a sense of profound peace and being at home with yourself.

Now return to your list and bring forward your top five. Here are some examples:

1 To be authentic
2 To be confident and lovingly assert myself
3 To have no barriers or conditions to love
4 To respect myself
5 To know what I want

Work with your own list or use these examples to give you a pattern you can follow to look at the issues that have come up for you. You may find that issues that previously you would have put top of your list no longer feature – enjoy the peace!

However, it's possible there are scars and blocks, old patterns and memories that are now rising to be healed. As you change your vibration so patterns that you release change too. Things that previously were important suddenly change in shape; healing happens quite instantly.

In your new energy and with your sense of completeness, is there one thing which links the issues on your list?

*****

## Love in motion

Make the sound of ohm or aum and listen and be aware of what is happening around you – keep in mind you have powers which are returning to you.

What is the sense you have? Call it a feeling, an awareness, a knowing.

There may be one thing which unites your list, and it's a belief, or maybe a series of memories and patterns that leave you with doubt that you can be loved without condition, that you cannot love yourself nor receive love from others unconditionally. Does this resonate with you?

Would you like to change this? How do you wish to change this?

Step back into your completeness and see if we walk beside

each other or if we are fellow travellers and now is the time for you to be experiencing the path that is you.

You have changed so much around you and your sense of what is real. Even now you can see that what before was real you have seen as illusion, and so you wonder if the new reality will also prove to be an illusion of a different kind. And then what does it matter? 'Being right' is part of the old baggage. Being you, vulnerable and powerful and love, is who you are.

**Your truth is eternal.** In your new reality it's time to connect with pure, unconditional love and to know that this is who you are. It's time for a miracle.

Find a quiet space and time. Sit or lie down comfortably.

From your feet if you are sitting, or from your heart center if you are lying down, send out roots to connect you with Lady Gaia and Sanat Kumara at the core of the earth.

From the crown of your head become aware of a thread which connects you to your guardian angel, the angels and ascended beings of great light, and to source, divine universal consciousness.

Bring your complete self into this healing - yourself as two halfs which are one. If it helps, repeat the exercise in which you brought together the two halfs of you.

Within this energy journey to the center of your heart. Find the still center of your heart. It is eternal, infinite, and pure, white light, all the colors of the rainbow in one light of wondrous intensity.

In the still center of your heart bring before you a white board, something you can write and draw on in large letters and words, or large symbols.

**Start writing and drawing** all of the things which now move before your awareness that block your connection to pure, unconditional love. Write them fast, whatever words come out, using whatever letters come to hand or whatever symbols and shapes appear. You will know them.

As you write and fill the board so will the board be cleansed. Allow the feelings that come with the words and letters and symbols and pictures to well up and flow. Some of the feelings and patterns will be condensed, others will appear individually, just allow them to be as they are.

What you are experiencing here is witnessing or observing. You are literally 'wiping your slate clean'; take as long with this part of your healing as you need. This is energy that can now be returned to you. To fast-forward the analogy from Victorian schooldays to current physical ways of communicating, you are deleting files and rebooting your capacity. The only addition to the analogy that is needed is that your capacity is not a static commodity like a memory stick, it is infinite.

When the flow of words, letters, symbols and pictures has stopped, direct that the white board be removed and move yourself deeper into the light.

If all around you is light **look for the focus of the light**, like the center of the beam, and walk along until you are completely at peace, exactly in the right place, in a state you have not experienced for a long, long time.

Direct that your heart open to the flow of this light. It is a flow of pure white and gold light. You are experiencing yourself as pure, unconditional love. See all petals, all layers, all the chambers of your heart opening and open to living in the flow of this love.

In this space meet whoever you wish and you will know them as they are. Beings of great light who work directly with the heart energies are Jesus, Mary Magdalene, Mother Mary, Krishna, Radha, Buddha, Babajii, Quan Yin, the Archangel Chamuel and Ganesh amongst others. You may wish to meet source, beloved mother, father God, beloved universal consciousness.

Ask of these loving beings anything you wish, or simply be in the energy.

There will be a time to return and you will know this for you have asked to live this life on earth and not to be continually in these energies, as wonderful as they are.

Take leave of your guides, giving them thanks and love and big hugs. Return back the way you came, back to your physical consciousness. Wiggle your toes and fingers and cup your eyes before opening them. Record your experiences.

*****

## How do you wish to experience life with another?

It's time for you to write your own script. What is your greatest dream of life with another?

What is it your heart asks to experience in this lifetime?

There was an interview with the actress Liv Ullmann for the Observer newspaper, Sunday 30th December 2007, and her answer to the question 'What does love feel like?' was

*'....when you feel free to say yes to whatever is best within you'.*

And now that you have experienced and reconnected to love what does it feel like? Are you free to say yes to whatever is best within you?

You may notice at this point that you have peace about lots of questions you may have started the game with, like should I stay with my current partner? Or maybe, is there a twin flame out there for me and should I make space for this flame to enter my life?

These are questions which are based upon a sense of you as incomplete; your questions now may be different. Because your heart is singing now do you wish to share that with another?

Ohm shanti, shanti, shanti.

*****

## Sex, power, sensuality and making love

It may be time to review at least some of the wonder of what it is to be  human as well spiritual in the same body.

The ways in which the terms sex, power, sensuality and making love are being used here may be different from those with which you are familiar so there is a short description of each term at the start of each section.

**Sex** is a function of the body, pleasurable or empty. It all depends on what else we are connecting to at the time. Think about sex on your own. Can you experience this as deeply pleasurable or is it shameful, or are you somewhere else on the spectrum? Perhaps sex on your own is a non-starter for you?

Wherever you are with this you can bring the duality of pleasure and shame into your triangle of experience. You are observing the duality but know that there is something permanent that this triangle flags up for you in your new reality. Think for a moment about shame; what is it? Get into the feeling of it, your own or the feeling you feel that others have carried, still carry to this day.

How do you get in touch with your feelings normally? If you access your feelings via your head then think about the role of shame. How and why has this feeling been used for years, centuries, across so many different cultures? Why has it been used to control women? How has that left things for men?

If you feel your way into your feelings then get into the pit of your stomach. Is shame a natural feeling? Hold the feeling and then illuminate it. What is it? Do you want it in your body?

You are currently co-creating your life so now is a good time to develop your new resources. How do you wish to deal with this feeling, this energy which hangs around being miserable and wretched? What are the **gifts** this energy brings which exist beyond the illusion? Do you wish to reach out for them to reclaim more of who you are?

How do you want to do this?

You'll be familiar with the way of the game and you are encouraged to work out the form of words that has resonance for you and reflects who you are:

Bring yourself, complete, into your present consciousness. Work out a form of words for releasing feelings which no longer serve you. Make it positive like 'I release' or 'I reclaim' or 'I direct'. For example

**Exchange:** 'I direct that this energy I have known as shame now leave all levels of my being. I direct that the gifts it presents, self-worth, be returned to me now, for I am love and I co-create with the divine'.

Witness the shift in these energies, the leaving of one and the filling of your being with the gifts that are the exchange.

If this shift has not occurred that's fine, you are simply bringing in and reclaiming more power. To do this get back into the feeling in your stomach or the indignation and sadness you created via your thoughts. Experience your feelings. Illuminate them. Call upon companions of the game to help if you wish.

Now drop through your feelings down to the next level. Where are you? Have a good look around. Get more light into the scene. There is nothing that you cannot illuminate, and nothing, no thing, that you cannot dissolve with your love. If you are still doubting your amazing powers or you would like some support whilst you focus on your feelings then call for help from Archangel Michael for you have felt his energy already and you know and are sure about his capabilities.

Where are you in the level below the feeling of shame? Bring more light in. Now see that you feel yourself to be trapped. This thing, shame, has made a prison for you, somewhere where you have existed, in a bizarre way somewhere where you have felt safe, but this prison no longer serves your purpose and no longer reflects who you are.

**Exchange:** It is time for change. Determine if there is more to do in this landscape. You will know. Feel the self-worth return to your body and from your body stimulate and change the aura, your energy field, around you.

See the fastenings on the bars loosening. Feel the grids and bars being lifted. And now they are gone. And what is flooding in is fresh air. What is flooding in is freedom and you are taking your first steps in a new reality and a new experience of you.

Form the words that are right for you for this moment. 'I am freedom and I reclaim my power.'

*****

## Power

With the word 'power' popping up as shame is released it may be timely to review power and where it fits in in the game in terms of intimacy.

In terms of 'old consciousness' power was the illusion of being stronger physically or 'coming out on top' because of human wilfulness, character and attitude, or possibly being more desirable – maybe where lust was concerned.

There might be all kinds of power imbalances due to age, social standing, economics, culture around marriage, gender, belief and faith systems, race, legislation, lack of self-worth and internal belief or fear systems amongst others.

As a duality, power seems to be there or not, powerful or weak, more powerful or less powerful. Why would this duality enter into intimate relationships?

Possibly for fear that without it basic needs might not be met; possibly as behaviour which is cultural or ancestral and has been observed in others, that this is the role, say, of the male and this the female; and then the role of power imbalance when we 'take it out on the other' i.e. sometimes the hurt we feel inside we express in anger, disdain, disrespect for another instead of dealing with those feelings.

**Applying the principles of the game** – that duality is an illusion and is offering us experience as well as a significant gift, an exchange, of permanent value and nature – what is it that we are learning from power within one-to-one or intimate relationships?

This feels like a good time to step firmly into your knowing of yourself as complete. Bring in power as a duality between which your experience has vacillated. As observer of the duality see what feelings the issue of power raises for you. Look to see if you have issues at either or both ends of the spectrum - at one end being ground down, powerless, abused, debased, worthless; at the other end triumphant, vindicated, powerful, confident.

**Go into the feelings,** taking each feeling one at a time and check this feeling of power or powerlessness. Does it feel natural? How does it compare to the feeling of power within your heart for instance? How has it served you to have had the experience of power within a spectrum of duality?

If there are aspects of these experiences that you now wish to release or exchange, form the words that bring you into your new consciousness of yourself. 'I release' or 'I reclaim' or 'I am' as examples.

'I release the feeling of being inadequate, being unable to defend myself, seeing no way through. I reclaim my power to love myself and my knowing that I am totally loved.'

And/or: 'I release the feelings of being victorious, confident, 'right' where this was at the expense of another. I reclaim my power to love myself and everyone else and my knowing that I am totally loved.'

How will you let this new form of power as love into your life and into your relationship(s)? It may help to form intentions about how you will deal with situations in future so that you will always know yourself as love.

*****

## Sensuality

Sensuality is being used here to describe a way of appreciating the love, beauty and light in another. It is expressed largely as a physical sensation, stroking, caressing, massaging. It encompasses the other physical senses too, taste, sight, smell, hearing, but also opens you to the non-physical self of yourself and others i.e. energy, love, light, soul.

Sensuality can be combined with sex or not.

A quick way back to sensuality is through touch. You can start on yourself first if you wish or find another and experiment with different ways of touching, say your foot or your lover's foot, or a hand. Try different pressures, different movements.

**Imagine that you have not touched a human body before**. Your finger tips are now sensors which are connecting you and through these you will know what a human body is. It may help to close your eyes so that the focus is on the sensations of touch and your other gifts of awareness.

Now open yourself to sensing all there is to know about this human body. What can you sense, what do you start to psychically know? Let more of these senses in.

Experiment with oil or cream and increase the pressure in your fingers and gently move the flesh underneath the skin. Sense how the flesh moves in ways which are natural and which bring energy and vitality to that area.

Imagine that your fingers are feathers and from the flesh you have massaged you are bringing back **sense and stimulation** to the very top of the skin so that the skin can tingle and refresh in every cell.

If you are experimenting with a partner with whom you are usually intimate, you might decide that you will learn about each other's bodies without the act of sex or making love. Agree that you will take time to know each other quite differently and ensure that you have time to enjoy connecting in this way, including time to hold.

Draw the curtains or use blindfolds to heighten the focus of senses other than sight. Experiment with being in nature, under the stars at night, down on the beach or in the woods and fields.

Talk afterwards about what you experienced. What caused your skin to tingle, the movement or sensations that you particularly enjoyed? What you would like to repeat or go on to, what made you feel connected and aware of yourself and the other person? How did this sense of connecting differently make you feel?

*****

## Making love

Making love is the bringing together of sensuality, power, sex and an openness to allow love. Love in the game is in three parts, and allowing love in includes love to receive, love for giving, and love to appreciate and honor. Allowing love invariably means that you have developed trust in yourself and that you are making full use of your discretion. Knowing what makes you feel good and knowing when someone else is on your wavelength.

Making love can also be a profoundly spiritual as well as a physical experience and when all elements are combined can provide experiences which feel other-worldly or totally blissful.

A good way to develop trust in yourself is to let go of hurt, slights, resentment and regrets. This is also a good process for bringing yourself into the present moment and for freeing up creativity.

Take a piece of paper and write down all the reasons **why you do not trust** yourself in intimate relationships. Everything. The faster you can allow the flow of words the better.

Next go back over your list and, starting at the top, for each reason you have put down see if there is a corresponding feeling somewhere in your body.

So for instance if you have put something down like, 'Because I got hurt the last time' see if there is a feeling which goes with this. Close your eyes if that helps to get focus on the feeling. Go into the feeling and see what it is.

Let's say that it's anger. Why? Because you knew it wouldn't last but didn't want to let go either. Who are you angry with? Yourself and someone else. Actually, now that you're in the feeling of it it's mostly this someone else.

Drop down from your feeling into the level below. What is there? Bring more light and illuminate this level. Ah, now you can see.

So it's time to release the baggage. 'I release this feeling of anger and rage and resentment towards X, realising s/he was acting out of love and doing the best they knew how. I release all regrets I have held since that moment. I reclaim my power. I am love.'

Work your way through your list. Use this exercise to become more in tune with who you are and who you know yourself to be. Answer the question 'I am........?' and get into the feeling of that quality as you clear old baggage and resentments.

If you find it difficult to feel the resentment - sometimes it is tucked away and not lively as feelings - then find a form of words that winkles the resentment out and clears your internal landscape of clutter, perhaps something like:

'I clear all resentments which have attached to these feelings of anger, along with the shock and trauma of the original events, and now sweep clean all clutter around these events. I trust myself'.

Remember to bring in the quality of trust. Once you trust yourself, your relationship to everyone else changes, significantly. This may feel like a detour on the road to making love and yet may be the key ingredient.

**Combining physical and spiritual energies in love:** within recent years there has been more awareness of forms of love-making which combine physical and sexual energies. The symbol for this form of union is the caduceus, two energies which wind around each other.

The energy is known as kundalini energy, and both as a physical sensation and spiritually kundalini energy sits at the base of the spine in the root chakra. During the act of making love the energy is raised and this can be done consciously or allowed to form naturally.

Because this is an act of becoming alive to each other and to the joining of energies, be sure that you are completely comfortable with each other. If there are issues of trust don't proceed – in truth your spiritual energies will not rise if there are blocks - this is a special ceremony.

**Make it a special ceremony.** Make the occasion joyful and sacred. In your preparations think about all of your senses which can include food and drink, your physical surroundings, music, all of the ways in which it is most wonderful to lift your vibration.

If your partner is using the same or similar spiritual language it can enrich experiences if you do some spiritual foreplay as well as physical - the meditation to cleanse the chakras which is in the warm-up exercises to the game for instance, and lead each other in this meditation, in love, appreciation and honoring of each other.

Physically it is traditional within this form of love-making for a male to sit cross-legged and for his partner to straddle him so that both partners are sitting upright and facing each other. Savour each moment and allow plenty of time for sensuality and foreplay before getting to this point.

The male sitting cross-legged penetrates his partner and the physical sensations begin to ripple from the root chakra up the spine to the crown of the head. As these sensations increase, the male sitting cross-legged can bring his awareness to his own root chakra and the warmth that is spreading around this area, like a ball of fire.

**For both partners,** allow this energy to rise, slowly at first and whilst the physical pleasure of making love continues. Become accustomed to the energy and allow for your partner to become aware of theirs too. Now bring your attention to each other and match your energies with those of your partner. Simply be aware of where the energy is with you and where it is with your partner and as your physical climax joins together so allow your spiritual climax to join too. Allow the two to become one, the physical and spiritual energies, both within yourself and then between yourself and your partner as one.

*****

## Soul Mates

The use of the term 'soul mate' can be found in use to describe people who are on a similar wavelength, through to very specific and codified beliefs about how souls were created and then how they were split up into families of souls and so on.

The way in which 'soul mate' is being used here is to describe people who share the same vibration or frequency. Our vibration is shaped and tempered, a little like the process of making steel, by how we have evolved, the life circumstances we have lived and how much light and love we have allowed to flow over many lifetimes.

Soul mates are therefore often those we have shared previous lifetime experiences with. It can be the case that we have contracted, in advance of taking our present lifetime, to share experiences and to act out roles for each other. These may not necessarily appear to be roles where love is demonstrated on the surface, which is why the gap or veil between love and enmity of those who have given us a hard time or abused us can be thin. Ultimately we are all here in love.

In consequence **once you have found completeness within,**

the quest or wish to find a soul mate subsides. It's likely that you have soul mates amongst your family and friends already. You'll know them because there is a bond between you, of love or enmity, which is somehow greater or deeper than usual or than you would otherwise expect. Sometimes these bonds are apparent when they have skipped a generation or there is someone within your family or someone you meet and you feel not only a profound love, but also a deep knowing about.

The same is true if a soul mate has taken an intimate relationship with you and having found completeness there is an opportunity to experience a depth of love which can be free from condition or conditioning. In such circumstances the key will be to remain in the present moment, for the depth of shared experience can unbalance soul mates as well as provide vast riches and depth.

*****

## Twin flames

If a soul mate vibrates at the same pitch as you then a twin flame replicates, exactly, your vibration. This can be deeply complementary, as in yin and yang energies, or contrarily can be deeply unsettling if you are so perfectly the same that there is no edge to your relationship.

As with soul mates, once you have found completeness within yourself the thirst or interest in finding your twin flame recedes. If you have some sympathy for the contention that we live at the root of our contradictions, then you'll allow that just as your interest recedes this is the moment when a twin flame or compatible soul mate is most likely to pop up.

*****

## The mystery and magic of love

If all of this were foretold and foreknown where would the mystery and the magic of love reside? We are here for the ride, for the mystery, the magic, the wonder, the splendour and beauty of love. For this reason we are separate, so that we can know the experience of that separateness when we come together as one, in romantic and spiritual union, or as one with all that is. These states of being are not opposed to each other. As we allow ourselves to know each, so something new can emerge. We can move or see through the duality of either, separate or one, and become something that is deeply both states at the same time and, because we have a third point of reference, something else beyond. And that is the third half of the game.

# 9

# Third half: finding everyone else

The game of the third half is played in extra time because it is optional. To take the option you'll have passion in your heart about your connection to spirit and about your love of life and living.

It's also a celebration of life. Just how fantastic it is to be authentic, to be free, to trust, to be vulnerable, to be open to all of the new experiences and the beauty of life and living.

## Death and dying

In a few cultures around the world there is a view that once we have the fear of death out of our system we can get on with living.

Such cultures have not made a large impact on a broad western culture where we tend to insure against our fears with doctors and hospitals, and hush up the dead and the dying – outwardly as a mark of respect for them.

Perhaps this is changing. All ossified and rigid structures, beliefs and fears eventually crumble. Our fear of death is no different.

With disconnection from universal consciousness, from the sense of who we are at a deep level, we came to fear the setting of the sun, to fear affliction, to see death as terminal and not within a cycle.

Possibly this goes hand-in-hand in the West with a retreat from nature into larger cities and industrialised lives. A cursory glance at nature reminds us that each season has its own part to play in a circle of creation, bloom and blossom, a colorful and serene letting go and death, to life being reborn.

Our own **innate feelings** serve to remind us that life in winter can be awesome, depths of stillness that are majestic.

There is something about dying to find life. In death there is a letting go - a surrender that allows life to continue. Perhaps we understand this from each other in ways that presently we do not articulate but which we 'get' on other levels. Perhaps those of us at the side of the death-bed learn from those in it that it's okay, it is alright to let go and let light.

**In terms of attachments** that we form and value in our lifetimes, life itself appears to be the attachment that it makes most sense to get in perspective. This is not a suggestion to walk out under a bus or look for other ways not to value life. It is more a case of surrendering our attachment to life so that we can live and value life.

Surrendering is the process of letting go of something that, until that point, you had invested a lot of energy in resisting, possibly with everything you had, and then embracing the very thing that you had resisted.

In death what is it that we resist? Imagine yourself with ten minutes to go and you are scanning the things that you are resisting. What are they? Make a list, allow your subconscious mind to raise the spectres and fears. Some things may be disguised but that's fine, you can see through the disguises.

How does your list compare with these suggestions?

Being vulnerable
Being in pain
Loss of control
Loss of dignity
Loss of our separateness, the things that make us unique
Saying goodbye to my children, not being there for my children
Saying goodbye to those I love
Giving up on roles I held for others

veils for death and dying are quite extraordinary gifts for living and so it's helpful to understand them a little more so that we can gain the lesson, cash in on the bonus material.

The question then becomes what is this attachment giving me, what is it I want to stop resisting and embrace?

Take the one that causes you the most emotion. Here's an example:

**Fear of the game being over,** that there is no more human life for you. You have dropped into the emotion and felt in the pit of your stomach an acute loss and this is sticky, tar-covered energy, and from this you drop through the emotion to the level below and find you are attached to life – a large cord fastens you to life on earth.

Bring your sense of yourself as complete into this present moment. Now form the words that resonate for you. 'I surrender to the game being over. I am the game being over. I embrace this aspect of myself for in surrender new life is born in me.'

Or maybe at the top of your list was **vulnerability.** Drop into the emotion and feel the feeling. Now drop through the feeling into the level below. What is here? Is there an attachment and what are you attached to?

When you are clear you are looking at the root cause, form your words. Something like:

'I surrender to vulnerability. I am vulnerable, I am vulnerability. All of this is in me. I embrace my vulnerability so that new life may grow'.

Understand yourself as the illusion and as the observer and now as all that is.

*****

### Who am I?

You'll recall doing this exercise in the section where you started to show up in your life. Don't refer back to the original exercise immediately because this time you can have a different experience of the question.

Ask the question of yourself, who am I? in such a way that you use the question as a process. This time you want to get into the awareness you have of yourself and it's not about having answers so much as a knowing.

Once you have the sense of this exercise and begin to experience who you are as an awareness you can intensify the quality or sense of what it is to be you.

Next, experiment with **being yourself and everything else**. This takes a few minutes where you allow yourself to merge. Because you are energy and everything else is energy make the intention that you will go lightly and ask permission at a spiritual level of the things you wish to merge with.

Start with things that are out in nature, a tree, a bird, a shrub or lawn for instance. To help the process describe how it feels to be this thing you have merged with. Allow your words to become a stream of consciousness about how it is to be the thing you have merged with.

**Experiment with size and scale**. Again ask permission. Merge with vastness, like the sky or the ocean, and describe how it is to be this wonderful panorama, how you feel, the things you care about. And then experience yourself as something that is tiny, an acorn perhaps or a plant seed. Describe how it is, get into the feeling of how it is.

You are all of this and more, and you are also separate. How else would you have the experience of love if your only consciousness was that you were love? This and more has been the gift of duality, the gift of your creation, the thing that you created.

*****

## Destiny and freewill

Where to next?

Do you wish to ascend or stay around for a while longer?

Destiny and freewill are a duality. They provide a spectrum of experience and then a lot more besides. It could be that they flag up for you the existence of an eternal truth, the finding of a quality that you have been looking for.

Following the rules of the game, both polarities are right for the experiences you have chosen and both exist to show that there is something else here, something that transcends the veils of illusion and speaks to a deeper truth.

For the moment go with this as a feeling or as an energy. It may exist for you like a vortex – a spiral or whirlwind of energy – or possibly a feeling of stepping through a door from one place to the next, which is also the same of course; you are in both places.

You know this and you know which place you wish to be in, or you know this but you want the game to go on.

*****

## Ascension

Ascension is optional.

If you are in any doubt about where you stand with ascension then work out if you wish to ascend, and, if yes, shine the light of your truth on your intention. Is there another issue which has ducked behind the label of ascension and which you now wish to gift to yourself?

We step down our vibration in order to live on earth and we raise our vibration to ascend. It used to be that the journey to ascension took a lifetime's commitment and possibly commitment over more than one lifetime. It is because some great souls made this commitment that we know that ascension is possible, that we know how to do it, and from these souls we can receive guidance on our own journey.

If you wish to ascend follow all of your instincts and internal prompts to raise your vibration and let go of worldly illusion. Some of this you have encountered in the games of the first and second half: the exercise in which you have recently seen through duality is where you will now wish to live for all of the days you choose to remain on earth.

Meanwhile **make your journey more comfortable** by clearing and cleansing internally and externally. Let go of all attachments. Clear out all baggage. Let go of all 'better than, worse than' duality, for the thing that will weigh you down more surely than anything else is internal judgement and feeling that you are more superior than or less superior than others.

This can be troublesome on a path that may look overtly spiritual to others for many will hold a mirror to you and say of you that you are special or somehow a great soul or more virtuous than others, and you would be advised to check out how words such as these make you feel in advance of your journey and checking to see what lies beneath if you find they strike a chord.

**If you choose to ascend** you will have the choice of whether you take your physical body or not. Your ability to do this will be enhanced by how light your body is. Not in weight and gravity terms but how light in energy.

Traditionally the way to lighten your body would be to spend long periods of time in communion with universal consciousness and great beings of light – in meditation – and look to maintain that consciousness for as many waking and sleeping hours as possible. The intention or drive behind ascension is invariably that your soul wishes to be reunited with spirit in as short a time as is possible.

Since 1987 it has been possible to bring more light and energy into our bodies in a magnified form, and changes since 1987 and particularly across 2009 have meant that the energy on earth has changed also. In consequence the time periods involved and the struggle or challenges that duality has presented have changed considerably too. It's more simple and it's faster to ascend.

You may have noticed that time has got quicker. This appears to be a shared experience. The energy has become lighter as more density has shifted in advance of a new dimension, an experience of fifth dimensional living being available on earth.

The consequence of all of this is that energy is available for ascension and the atmosphere around you has shifted making ascension easier. Having said all of this keep in mind that you are also human, and energy shifts, whilst having speeded up considerably, are still in line with what you can take as a human being.

The most recent changes in energy signal the return of divine feminine energy. In the west we might associate this energy with Mary Magdalene, in the East with Quan Yin.

To access the energy of the divine feminine find a quiet space and time. Sit or lie down comfortably ensuring that your back is straight. Close your eyes.

From the soles of your feet send down roots to the core of the earth. Here you ask that they are anchored to life-giving crystals by Lady Gaia and Sanat Kumara. Form the intention that you will connect with feminine and masculine energies which support and nourish your journey here as a human being, and bring those energies up from the earth into your chakra system, and up as far as your heart.

From the crown of your head feel the thread that connects you to your guardian angel, and thereafter to great beings of love and light, and to source, universal consciousness. Here connect with divine feminine and divine masculine energies which support and nourish your journey as an amazing spiritual being. Bring these energies down as far as your heart and let them gently merge with energies from the earth.

Make the intention that you will welcome the return of the divine feminine energy with a statement like "I open to receive and anchor the return of the divine feminine energy. I am in divine flow"

Draw down as much of the rebalanced energies as you feel you need each day.

If you had a light meter you'd see that you are simply becoming lighter. Allow time to assimilate the energy, say giving yourself a sleep cycle before charging up with more.

On the ascension journey you will find that additional guidance arrives in the form of knowing. You know yourself to be love, and all around to be love, and your connection to universal consciousness and nearness of the beloved will simply expand exponentially.

It could be you choose to slip away from earth whilst in an altered state or that you make the decision consciously. You may take your body with you or leave it behind.

Om mani padme hum.

*****

## A new way of being

If you've had a look at your options and decided you're sticking around then it's likely that you're here to help bring in and anchor a new consciousness, a new dimension on earth for a new way of being. How do you feel when you read these words?

The consciousness or energy in which we all move in the world today is quite different from that of 50 years ago, and it's likely that in another 50 years our way of being will have changed full circle.

**The year 2012** is a date which has stood out for some time amongst those who prophesise the future. It is the date when things change to such a degree that what lies beyond is something radically different. This is the date where one Mayan calendar stops and a new one begins. This is the date at which there is a pause between the in-breath and the out-breath of

Brahma according to ancient Hindi texts, a cycle which takes 26,000 years to complete. It looks like the time when the world ends and the new world begins.

You are here having chosen to play extra time; what do you feel? Is it doom and gloom or the birth of heaven on earth? And then if the question is polarised, what is the eternal truth that is gifted to us? How you feel about these questions will be important for you are the one you've been waiting for.

The new dimension is called the **fifth dimension**. The third dimension is where we lived on earth and a strong energy of this would have been around about 50 years ago, being a very physical and material consciousness. The fourth dimension is the energies we are living in at the moment. This is where the awareness of unconditional love and the knowing that we are unconditional love are able to be supported. We are able to 'go with the flow' and let go and let light. This is also a time when angels have reappeared in our individual and collective consciousness and we are able to see and sense beyond the veils of the physical world to realities or visions beyond.

Energies of the fifth dimension are already with us and support us in our ability to co-create with the divine. We are able to draw on those energies for clearing and healing issues which no longer serve us; reflect on how quickly things have cleared and healed for you within the game. We are also able to draw in new energies to sustain and support the return of powers and wisdoms which have lain dormant within the worlds we do not see but that are now opening to us.

These energies bring together the return of divine feminine energies in balance with divine masculine energies. You are both of these energies but in polarity we may have been in the habit of seeing one energy or the other 'on top' or more to the forefront.

**The building blocks of creation:** dropping polarity gives us not only masculine and feminine together, but something new, somewhere we have not been for a long time. In our understanding it might equate to the saying that the whole is greater than the sum of its parts – but this saying does not adequately describe what is happening. What are available are the building blocks of creation.

How to experience this energy:

Find a quiet space and time. Sit or lie comfortably and switch off the phones. Close your eyes. Become aware of yourself as complete, being physical and spiritual and raise your vibration. Direct that you become more of yourself and intensify this light.

**Fifth dimensional energies:** see before you a flame. Bring the flame to life-size and see the colors of the flame as gold, silver and violet. These colors permeate the flame and energise the flame. This is an energy and the flame has no capacity to burn. These energies and colors prepare you for receiving fifth dimensional energy. When you are ready step into the flame and feel the energy of gold, silver and violet cleansing your aura and the energy space around you.

Now feel this flame divide into three parts. The bottom third shoots from the soles of your feet down to the core of the earth, blazing the way for your roots to the core of the earth to be strong, cleansed and anchored. Ask that your roots be anchored with Lady Gaia and Sanat Kumara and listen for a 'click' or sense the confirmation that you are anchored in feminine and masculine energies.

The top third of your flame moves from the crown of your head and now blazes the way for your connection to be strong and cleansed via your guardian angel and great beings of love and light all the way to source, universal consciousness and all that is. Ask to connect and anchor your being with the divine feminine and masculine energies of the beloved. Listen for a 'click' or sense the confirmation that you are anchored.

The remaining third of the flame now cleanses you internally. Become aware of the flame entering your energy system at some distance below the soles of your feet, clearing and cleansing and making strong your anchor to the earth's energy grid. From here the colors and energy of the flame - gold, silver and violet - move through your body to the root chakra, where they bring fresh color, vibrancy and power.

**The connections between your chakras** are also being cleansed so take your time with the flame and allow it to blaze and cleanse. From your root the flame spirals to your sacral chakra where it refreshes and awakens new creativity and joy for life.

From your sacral the flame moves to your solar plexus. In this area there can be a lot of emotion: feel the reconnection here between your power, yourself as love, and the peace and harmony of knowing that you are safe and balanced with this power. Enjoy this feeling. The gold, silver and violet flame moves next along the connections between your solar plexus and your heart.

At your heart center bring more of the gold in your flame forward and let it bring sustenance to your heart. Your heart has waited for this moment and is now opening to more love, to more life, to more of who you are as a multi-dimensional being. Allow the flame to sparkle and make this a celebration.

From the heart the flame travels to your throat chakra. Along the way there is a chakra which is opening to connect with universal love and all that is. This chakra is mid-way between your heart and your throat. It is sometimes called the $8^{th}$ chakra. You may sense the colors here as aqua-marine or turquoise. Allow this chakra to open gently and let the flame gently tickle the petals or gently spin the wheel of this emerging energy center.

From the $8^{th}$ chakra the flame proceeds to your throat. Here you speak your truth and articulate who you are. Let the gold, silver and violet colors vibrate in your throat area, a little like gargling water, but with the vibration of the color. Next the flame travels, cleansing and clearing your connection to your third eye.

Bring more focus to your third eye so that your new landscape can appear in ways that will also be familiar to you. Let the flames bathe the eye bringing new energy and vitality and more clarity. From the third eye the gold, silver and violet flame moves to your crown chakra.

The crown chakra is your gateway to source. Here the **flames dance**. Ask that in the flames any remaining barriers to your connection with source, universal consciousness, and all that is be cleared and transmuted. These can be thoughts or feelings that surprise you - simply let them go in the bonfire of being.

There are chakras which exist outside your physical body; allow the flame to dance through these, rising to three or four feet above your head before you see the flame re-engage with the other two parts of the flame becoming one whole flame. Reduce the flame in size so that it can burn gently just in front of you, available for you to brush any remaining thoughts or blocks into the flame for transmutation.

Take your awareness to the soles of your feet and your roots which stretch all the way down to the core of the earth. Feel your connection to Lady Gaia and Sanat Kumara and increase the depth of your connection.

**Balance your energies:** direct that the energies of masculine and feminine on earth from Lady Gaia and Sanat Kumara join together and travel up your roots in balance. This balanced energy, representing the energy of you as a human being, travels through the soles of your feet and through your energy system up to your heart.

Here in your heart the energy gives creation to something that is the feeling of both energies and also new. This is you as a human being.

Now take your attention to your connection to spirit and the great beings of light, and all that is. From this energy you were created as a spiritual being and you draw down the energies of your spiritual creation, divine feminine and divine masculine in balance, from source, through your crown chakra, your third eye, throat chakra and into your heart. In your heart the energies of divine feminine and divine masculine join so that you feel both energies and also a new energy, which is you as a spiritual being.

You are here in human form and you are here as an amazing spiritual being. You have brought both halfs of yourself together. In doing so you are in the process of creating something that goes beyond the sum of these parts, something that is one with these energies but also something that is new and newly created.

You are co-creating with the divine and you are bringing a new way of being into your life and into the world with a new experience of you. Welcome, you are the one you've been waiting for.

When you are ready allow the energies from earth which have joined in balance and are now in your heart to join with the energies from spirit which have joined in balance in your heart.

You will know this as the process of creation and the process of creating a new energy. When one and two join together they make one, but also a third, together and separate. This is your gift to the world and this is an expression of your love.

Stay in these energies and when you are ready to return bring these energies with you.

To return to your awareness of physicality bring your attention back to your breath and take three deep breaths. On the third breath direct that you will return to your physical body, feeling the effects of gravity on your body, wiggle your toes and fingers and in your own time open your eyes.

Welcome to your new way of being.

This is the end of the game and the start of a new cycle, but pause awhile, for in stillness you will know your soul, and in knowing your soul you will know all others – and it is to know and experience your soul and all others that you came.

# 10

# Conclusion

For a refreshing cup of tea:

Take about 10 fresh mint leaves
One fifth of a red chilli pepper, de-seeded and chopped
Add to a large tea pot with lots of boiled water
Leave to brew

If you have a plate warmer or a stand for the pot with space for a small candle beneath the pot then add boiling water to the pot as and when and keep this brew going for the day.

Thank you for your company and this journey we have taken together. Go well, and may the peace of the angels be with you.

Namasté

# Appendix i) The short game

The short game is written for readers who are short of time or who wish to dip their toe into the style of finding your other half.

There are rules to the game and instructions on how to play. For the short game the golden rule is to be yourself: if you're looking for your other half how will that other half know you if you are pretending to be somebody else?

There are three halfs to find. The first half to find is the other half of yourself. In shorthand this is your spiritual self, the part of you that you cannot see but can sense. Having found yourself the second half is to find a partner and romance (should you wish to do so) and thereafter the third half, played in extra time, is to find everyone else.

So what does **the first half**, this other half of yourself look like, and where are you likely to find this other half?

Come on out to play. Start with a game of **hide and seek**. To get into the game you'll need to play along for a minute or two. Find a quiet time and space and close your eyes and count to 20 and then announce that you're coming, ready or not. And have a look. Oh and keep your eyes closed.

What you find may be surprising. Maybe an energy? Maybe light or other colors? Essentially the other half of you is many of the things that you can't see with your naked eye but that you are aware of beyond your normal physical senses, what you feel in your gut, or your **intuition**. Your intuition is the key to your heart and the other half of you includes what you know in your **heart** to be your truth, as well as what you are aware of in your **soul**.

If you're not yet into the game try this. It can help to do this with your eyes closed simply because when your eyes are open your brain engages, and the other half of you is not your brain. This takes a minute. In front of you is a road or highway with two lanes. It's going in one direction. You are in the left-hand or inside lane. You are aware that the outside lane, the right-hand lane, is empty. When you are ready drop into the outside lane. That's it. In this space ask to know more of yourself.

If you're ready to invite more of this other half into your life you may need to prepare the way. There's a chance that you have a war going on and if this is the case it's hard to invite somebody into your life when you're at war. So **declare an amnesty** and make peace with yourself.

It can help if the amnesty is simple, something like 'I now declare an amnesty and will allow myself to be at peace with myself'. You may need a peace process to give full effect to your peace declaration and in this regard it helps to decide what it is you are now ready to forgive and release about yourself. Be specific. Write it down and let it go. Keep in mind that at any point in your life you were doing the best you knew how with what was going on. You have not missed the bus. You did not take a fatal wrong turn 5 years ago. You are in exactly the right place at the right time. You are perfect as you are. Enjoy the peace dividend.

There is an **exchange principle** going on in your life. It works something like this. When you find out who or what is pressing your buttons and drop into the emotion which is below the surface emotion you can not only release the emotions, all of them, but get an exchange and get back the **quality you were seeking**. It may help if there's an example.

On the surface you're exasperated with your daughter. She knows exactly how to wind you up, she can do it with a glance or a tone of phrase. So you stop and wonder where the exchange is. You drop below the exasperation and look for the emotion below the surface. What is here? It's a little girl who was trying to express herself and she was shut up each time she spoke her truth. It's quite possible she looks a little frightened, maybe a little lost or neglected. She looks like you. She is you. What is it she needs? She needs to know it's okay to come out and be herself and that she is safe, that you are now the adult and that you will take care of her and that she is loved for who she is. If this feels right bring her into your heart and let her know she is loved. You will notice that you feel different after this. You have exchanged exasperation for the experience of being loved unconditionally. Your relationship with your daughter will also change.

Take all opportunities to swap the blocks and hang-ups in your life for the qualities that you came here to experience and enjoy.

Another way to bring more of your other half consciously into your life is to look at life using a different perspective or through a different lens. **When you dissolve duality** you also dissolve fear. This way of thinking can take a little while to accommodate. It may help to think of duality as a tool by which we get experience. Something is too hot or too cold, tall or short; there is plenty for everyone or there will never be enough. To get the experience of too much or too little we are also in the position of observing this one thing or another. So there are not two things going on but three, and the third is how we experience, by observing or taking part. It may help to have an example: we persuade ourselves that love is conditional: he loves me because of this, she doesn't love me because of that. Yet if we think about it for a moment the conditions we place on this love of hers or his are of our making. We can't know what is going on for someone else only what we are feeling. The upshot of this is that we are in control of how much love we choose to experience.

It follows from this that a quick way to get our sense of ourself as being **whole and complete** might be to open up to more love. On the basis that if we've been looking and maybe longing for more to life and we've been rationing this love, maybe love without condition is what is missing.

This can be scary as well as fun so check out how you are feeling. When you are ready, form the intention that you will **open your heart** to **receive and allow** more love into your heart and into your life.

If this feels good, form the intention that you are ready and willing to allow more love to flow into your heart **for giving**. This may sound cheesy but it's true. Love for giving is love forgiving. Forgive yourself also.

Finally what brings this love to life, i.e. you get a feel for being able to live and operate within this energy, is forming the intention that you will open your heart to **love to honor** and appreciate. Start slowly and build up. Think of a role model, someone who supported you, cared for you, without condition. Let the appreciation start there. From there you can remember the rest of life. How fabulous life is. How great other people are. The generosity of strangers. How wonderful nature is. How gorgeous you are.

Once you have the sense of being complete again, feeling whole and taking responsibility for your life, then **finding romance with someone else** is easy-peasy. You have a much clearer sense of what is you and what is them. In this way you can open to the wonder of sharing love with another from a position of love rather than fear, of security rather than insecurity, of appreciation rather than mistrust.

**If you are single:** to get a quick sense of who you are looking for, this other half that is another person, close your eyes and feel yourself as a ball of light. You want to attract a ball of compatible energy. Ask for the energy of the person who is best suited to you as a partner and ask to experience their energy here with your eyes closed. Be clear about yourself as an energy and be clear about this other person as a separate energy, and if it feels right direct that the two balls merge for a moment and then separate again. In this way you can know your future partner as an energy signature – and you will know them when you meet in physical form.

**If you are in a committed relationship:** take some time out to work out why you have met and why you are making a life together. Look to see where the exchange is, the qualities you wish to experience, and the many opportunities that your partner is bringing to you to experience these. Look to see what it is you can bring into your partner's life, in love, for your partner's best experience.

A question that may help define how you wish to live your life in relationship with another: **Are you free to say yes** to all that is **best** about you?

**Take your relationship further** and list what you want in your relationship and what you do not. Every relationship in your life to date will serve you, even those where you were an observer rather than an active participant. List all the things you don't want in a column down the left-hand side of a piece of paper. Keep an eye on your emotions. The items where you get the most emotional connection are usually the most important to you.

Let's say you have one or two of the following: dishonesty, pretence, disrespect, disinterest, not being loved, feeling I've got to make the other person happy, a partner who doesn't know what they want.

Now in a column next to the first column translate each item that you don't want into something you do want and write it in such a way that it becomes active and positive about yourself. For instance

| I don't want | I do want |
|---|---|
| Dishonesty | To be honest |
| Pretence | To be authentic |
| Disrespect | To respect myself |
| Not being loved | To love myself |
| Being responsible for another's happiness | To take responsibility for my own happiness |
| A partner who doesn't know what they want | To know what I want |

If you follow your emotions and intuition with this list and follow through on the exchange that is offered you will have the tools with which you can deepen and extend your relationship(s). This will be in all relationships. You now have a list of qualities that are about you. Be the qualities, allow them into your life.

## Power and sensuality

Intimate relationships are a fantastic place to remember all the good things about you and to share and experience these through the eyes and senses of another.

Having found your spiritual self you'll be aware that you were created of **feminine and masculine energies** on earth and in spirit, and for these two halfs of yourself to be created it required that both of these energies were present and balanced. When these energies join together, in balance, something new can be created. You, for instance.

Understanding this balance means that any power imbalance in relationships shows up quickly. Misuse of power usually represents fear. Fear is part of a duality that helps serve us and we can look for an exchange. Do a swap. One leads to another, without one we do not find the other, i.e. identifying a power imbalance and recognising that this imbalance no longer serves you can help to flag up the quality that you now wish to experience. Maybe what you do wish to experience is the power of love?

It can help to change the rules. Maybe invest in the **sensual side** of your relationship as a way back to balance. What about sensuality without sex? Making time and space to explore each other as if you were discovering a human body for the first time? Or maybe using your fingers as if they were feathers? Using oils or creams to explore gentle ways of massaging and caressing, feet, hands, scalp, shoulders, as a means to engage and be with each other on a different level?

**Finding everybody else** in the game heralds a new approach to what we have known previously as ascension. There is a new consciousness available to us on earth and being born on earth and in spirit you are completely equipped to help birth and anchor this new energy.

A quick introduction to finding everybody else is to close your eyes. See or sense yourself as a **ball of light** or energy. Sense everybody and everything else as energy. When you are ready and have the sense of yourself as being separate, ask that you merge with the energy or light of everybody and everything else and when you are ready bring yourself back as separate and decide that you will return to your physical body.

Another variation is to take yourself out into nature. Focus on a tree. Soften your focus and ask permission for your energy and the energy of the tree to merge. Now try smaller things, a flower for instance. And then experiment with larger things like a river, or the sky. Find a friend who would like to play this game and ask if you can merge with their energy.

This is on the road to oneness, and because in life things have a habit of coming full circle, the road to oneness is found by recognising yourself. You are the path.

This is the end of the short game. If you'd like to check your progress and see how you did you'll need a pen or pencil - colored pencils are good - and 2 minutes to doodle. Simply sketch or doodle what you become aware of. The more of you that shows up the more of you you will doodle. In this way you will know when you are complete because your space will be complete and will feel coherent.

In the same way, if there are parts that have yet to be found or if the picture feels unbalanced or not quite right, then play the longer version of the game. You will have a sense of what is missing and what needs working on because your picture will reflect this for you, and invariably it means you are saving a treat or two for yourself.

Here's the doodlegram: you are invited to draw whatever feels right, both as to the representation of your physical self and your other half.

**Doodlegram**

My physical self | My other half

You may find that, as more of you shows up on the right of your doodle, how you represent yourself physically can change too – for as we become more aware of our other half and allow more of that into our lives so our physical body becomes more healthy and balanced.

Namasté

# Appendix ii) Chakra meditation

This meditation is referred to at two points in the game and so is printed here for ease of reference.

The meditation is designed to cleanse the chakras – your energy system – so that the energy points themselves are opened to a gentle flow of energy and so that the connections between the points are eased and unblocked.

Once this is done the meditation includes the opportunity to rebalance energies, masculine and feminine, using energies available here on earth and energies from spirit, and in this meditation you can know yourself as a bridge between spirit and matter.

**Find a quiet space and time.** Close your eyes and bring your awareness back to yourself with one or two breaths.

Now imagine a candle flame in front of you. On the outside it is composed of three primary colors. These are gold, silver and violet. Allow the flame to get larger until it is life-size. Let the flame become a flame of light and vibration, and take away the capacity of this flame to burn and when you are ready see yourself stepping into it.

In your mind's eye the flame envelops you. Feel or sense it cleansing and stay in this life-size flame for one or two minutes. It's possible you will start to feel lighter and maybe notice the change in the air around you which can become lighter and sweeter.

Once you feel that energies around you have changed ask that your life-size flame divide into three parts.

**Grounding:** the first part you send from the soles of your feet down into the ground to blaze and clear a connection which you are making with the energy at the core of the earth. The flame will blaze a path and clear your connection with the earth's core.

You are connecting with energy which creates matter. You

may know this energy as Lady Gaia or mother earth and Sanat Kumara, or the green man. These energies are masculine and feminine and they are joining to create a new balanced energy.

Now bring your attention to the top third of your flame.

**Connecting:** ask that this third of the flame move from the crown of your head along the connection you have to your higher self and from your higher self to your guardian angel, your spirit guides, and to source, the creator, universal consciousness and all that is.

You are connecting to a new light and a source of energy which is being returned to the earth after a long absence. It is a balance of male and female energies. You may sense these as Jesus Christ and Mary Magdalene, or as Krishna and Radha, or Yin and Yang or beloved mother, father God.

Now bring your attention to the middle and remaining part of the flame. Ask or direct that this flame move within your body to cleanse, clear and stimulate your energy or chakra system.

**Cleansing the chakras:** Bring the remaining part of the flame to a point about two yards, or 180 cms below your feet. Bring in the colors of gold, silver and violet to the flame. Now see the flame move to the soles of your feet – your feet move you through life – and from your feet to the energy points at your knees - which provide movement as well as the ability to hold your ground – and from your knees to the first of the 7 major chakras which is your root chakra at the base of your spine.

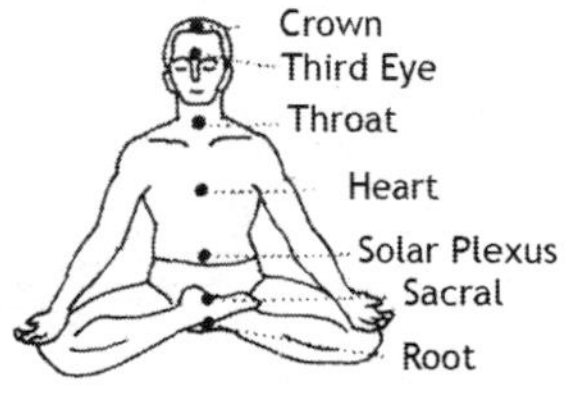


The **root** energy point provides much of our grounding as spiritual beings in human form and it is in this place in our energy system that we know when we feel safe and secure.

Let the flame stay here whilst it cleanses and gently starts to open your chakra. The color of this chakra is usually a deep red and the flame will cleanse any shadows or flecks.

It is important to pay attention to the connection between your chakras, i.e. the thread or column which connects your energy system along which the flame of light moves and along which the new energy will move.

From your root chakra move the flame along to your **sacral** which is the width of two fingers below your tummy button. The sacral is the energy of sociability, community, and also stores the energy for much of our creativity including our sexual and sensual nature. The color of this chakra is usually orange.

Again take time for the flame to cleanse and rejuvenate the energy point. At any of the chakras the flame may move through quickly or may stay awhile to cleanse and clear. Simply allow the process to achieve what it needs for you.

From your sacral move the flame along to the **solar plexus** which is just below the ribcage and at the top of your stomach. In the solar plexus we hold many of our emotions including emotions which we have denied or otherwise repressed. The color of this chakra is usually yellow or gold. The solar plexus is also where we find or determine our courage and integrity.

Allow the flame to cleanse and clear the passage or route from the sacral to the solar plexus and allow time at the solar plexus to cleanse and for the flame to gently rotate or move the energy.

Sometimes the connection between the solar plexus and the heart can become blocked so be aware of the progress of your flame and of where it needs to stop and take longer to refresh your system.

The **heart** is love. It is our connection to source and all there is. The heart knows love to be infinite but our experience as humans is to regulate this love.

Whilst the flame is cleansing your heart consider whether you wish to adjust the regulation of the flow, perhaps to receive a little more and to give a little more love and to allow more love into your life by honoring and blessing. The color of the heart is usually pink on the outside and green at the center.

From your heart the flame will move along to the energy point in your throat. Note, there is a turquoise blue between the heart and the throat which appears to be a combination of the heart green and the throat blue and signifies a connection or expression of **universal love**. This is sometimes referred to as the 8th chakra; allow your flame to gently play with the petals of this chakra before moving on.

Allow the flame to cleanse and clear and revitalise your system and to move gently up to the **throat chakra**. This is where we speak our truth and express our identity. The color of the throat chakra is usually blue which can range from a mild or soft blue through to an intense cobalt blue. Experiment with 'gargling' using the colors of the flame.

The next energy point is your **third eye** through which we develop our sense of the psyche, i.e. unseen energies and the spiritual. The color of this chakra is usually indigo or a deep navy blue. The third eye can appear in a variety of shapes, perhaps as a diamond with many facets or simply as an eye.

Finally the **crown chakra** is usually pure or pearlescent white and purple. The crown regulates the flow of spiritual energy from source, the creator, all that is.

Allow the flame to continue from your crown chakra upwards for about three feet so that it may take in energy centers which are outside your physical body, and then bring all three parts of the flame together and reduce the size of the flame.

Next send the flame back down your roots to the core of the earth. From this connection ask that balanced **masculine and feminine energies** from Lady Gaia and Sanat Kumara gently ascend through your roots and through your energy system up to your heart. Take a moment to experience this energy.

Next send the flame from the crown of your head to source, universal consciousness, and ask that balanced male and female energies of **divine love** descend and enter your energy system, descending as far as your heart. Take a moment to experience this energy and the feel of how it is to be in the combined energies.

Stay for as long as you like. Remember you can come back here anytime you like and you can bring these wonderful energies into day-to-day life with you as you return.

To **return,** become aware of yourself held in the energies of the flame, the colors and vibration of gold, silver and violet. Step backwards, away from the flame until you see the flame as you did at the start of the exercise and reduce it in size.

Now determine to come back into your physical body and feel your feet and fingers, giving your toes a wiggle, your fingers a wiggle, feeling your physical self sitting on the chair or lying down with the effects of gravity on your body, and in your own time open your eyes and return to your physical space.

Take a drink of water and record any impressions.

# Appendix iii) Opening to love

Beloved source, universal consciousness, all that is:

I open my heart to love to receive: to receive your blessings, your support, your love.

I open my heart to love for giving: to thank you for this day, this journey, this flow of love, this experience.

I open my heart to love to appreciate and honor: to honor the truth, beauty, valour and love in myself and all I share this wonderful life with.

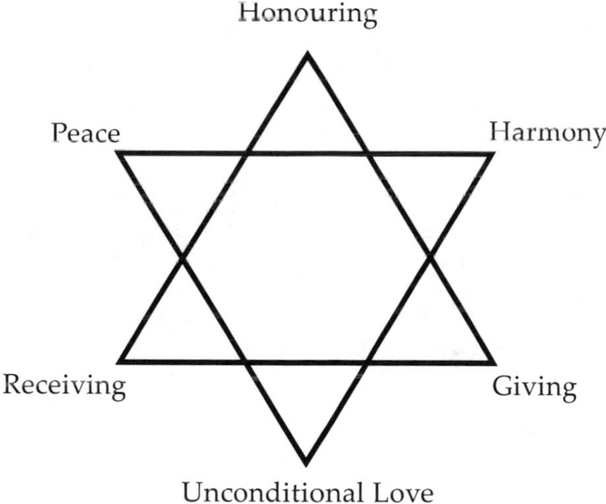


May these acts of giving, receiving and honoring merge with your peace, harmony and unconditional love so that I may know heaven on earth
in this moment and all days.

So be it, it is done.

# Appendix iv) Out-takes

(Channelled writing) "What is here? All that you have dreamed of and more. And the countless dreams of others. Is it very beautiful, no? Yes. From yes comes beauty, from no comes nothing. It is exact. Say yes to life and give life to the smallest, tiniest seed and the largest mountain. Say yes, give life. What a life!

Words are limited. You all know this - but still persist! It was also spoken of in Conversations with God. Thoughts are way more exact than words because they carry light as well as vibration. This is why we are advised to pay heed to our thoughts.

All of these things we know and we don't. There is knowing and there is experiencing. It will please you to take notice of the experiencing. As a generalisation, you thirst for knowledge and pursue knowledge but your heart yearns for experience.

We're not wistful for something we've had. Wistful is wishing we had let the moment enter. To let the moment enter breathe deeply and let it enter your heart. What follows is appreciation, and that is a glow. You do not miss something that you have appreciated."

The hardest lessons to learn are the hardest lessons to learn because they are the hardest lessons to learn. They are your greatest gifts.

*"At a certain point we forgive because we decide to forgive. Healing occurs in the present, not the past. We are not held back by the love we did not receive in the past, but by the love we're not extending in the present."*

Marianne Williamson "A Return to Love" p.175

*"...I wondered if that was how forgiveness budded, not with the fanfare*

*of epiphany, but with pain gathering its things, packing up, and slipping away unannounced in the middle of the night."*

Khaled Hosseini "The Kite Runner" p.313

*"Yoga isn't about standing or lying on a mat.*
*It's about learning to be fearless in your life"*

Rozz, yoga teacher , el jardin encantado, near Malaga, Spain.

(Channelled writing) New steps to spirit: "In the beginning the only word that was needed was ohm. Aum. Ohm is better, more O at the beginning. Ohm. It carved through rock, it made the tiniest seed feel good and grow. Life from a speck, life from mountains. Now the word is neglected and there are so many other words none of them with the same impact. Do not forget this.

We live in different worlds and yet we can overlap. You do with me and I do with you. How we communicate is by spirit. The more you listen to your spirit the more you can listen to spirit.

Where to find your spirit? It is not an exact science because you can all find it in different ways. Largely in the silence of the heart, but also in the third eye. The intention to listen to spirit is the best first step. There are others of course. It can be a hang-up for you – humankind – that things have to be done a particular way.

Ohm with love for 10 minutes.

What is love? Ultimately it is everything, for the world you know is made with love. But for now think of saying thank you for something you appreciate and transfer this feeling into your ohm. Say thank you for life – for beauty – for color – for the love of another human being.

It's quite therapeutic too? Now listen for 10 minutes and discern. Discern always.

Clarity is a return to stillness."

# Appendix v) Books and soundtrack

Barack Obama *The audacity of hope* first published 2006 by Crown Publishers USA, & 2008 Canongate Books Scotland

Claire Scobie *Last seen in Lhasa* 2006 Rider Books, England

Diana Cooper *A little light on the spiritual laws* 2000 Hodder & Stoughton, England

Diana Cooper *A new light on Ascension* new edition 2007 Findhorn Press, Scotland

Eckhart Tolle *A New Earth* 2006 Penguin Books, England

Gill Edwards *Living magically* 1991 Piatkus reprinted 2000, England

Javier Moro *The mountains of the Buddha* 2000 Full Circle, India

Khaled Hosseini *The kite runner* 2003 Bloomsbury, England

Levi *The aquarian gospel of Jesus the Christ* 1964 Fowler, England

Marianne Williamson *A return to love* 1996 revised edition Thorsons, England

Marshall Govindan *Babaji and the 18 siddha kriya yoga tradition* 1991 Kriya Yoga Publications, Canada

Paul Brunton *A search in secret India* Original copyright 1935. Revised edition 1985 by Weiser Books, USA

Paramhansa Yogananda *Journey to self-realisation volume III: discovering the gifts of the soul* 1997 Self-Realisation Fellowship, USA

Paramhansa Yogananda *The essence of Kriya Yoga* 2006 Alight Publications, USA

Ram Alexander *Death must die* (based on the diaries of Atmananda who followed a life-long spiritual journey with Shree Anandamayee Ma) 2000 Indica Books, India

Swami Rama *Living with the Himalayan masters* 1978 & 1999 Himalayan Institute Press, USA

## Soundtrack

Music, like many things, such as art, dance, poetry, clean air and cooking done with love can help us to bridge the world between the invisible and the visible, between spirit and matter, and help to sustain our soul. The following are tracks or albums which have helped me to express some part of the game and may have filtered into the game.

**Afro Celt Sound System Vol 1 : Sound Magic** by the Afro Celt Sound System

**Celestial Sounds** by Rosemary Stephenson featuring crystal singing bowls and overtones

**Journey to the Christ Light** by Edwin Courtenay and Rosemary Stephenson. A meditation to activate the higher chakras with color, light and sound

**Love Tattoo** by Imelda May

**Mess Around** by Ray Charles

**Refuge** by Gabrielle Roth & the Mirrors, featuring the chants of Boris Grebenshikov and synthesizer by Harvey Jones

**Sym.pa.thy** by daisyb, her first cd with four tracks

**The Essence** by Deva Premal

**The very best of Nina Simone** - the whole album and especially the track 'I wish that I knew how it would feel to be free'

**Tribal Nation** by Medwyn Goodall and the percussion of Scott Jasper

**U2 The Best of 1990 – 2000** and particularly the tracks 'One' and the new version of 'Numb'.

BOOKS

O is a symbol of the world, of oneness and unity. In different cultures it also means the "eye," symbolizing knowledge and insight. We aim to publish books that are accessible, constructive and that challenge accepted opinion, both that of academia and the "moral majority."

Our books are available in all good English language bookstores worldwide. If you don't see the book on the shelves ask the bookstore to order it for you, quoting the ISBN number and title. Alternatively you can order online (all major online retail sites carry our titles) or contact the distributor in the relevant country, listed on the copyright page.

See our website **www.o-books.net** for a full list of over 500 titles, growing by 100 a year.

And tune in to myspiritradio.com for our book review radio show, hosted by June-Elleni Laine, where you can listen to the authors discussing their books.